Pay Off Your Debt for Good

21 days to change your relationship with money & improve your spending habits so you can get out of debt fast

By Jen Smith

PAY OFF YOUR DEBT FOR GOOD

ISBN 978-1-7016-7151-5

YOUR FREE GIFT

As a special bonus, I've made a workbook to help you conquer the next 21 days of action steps.

The workbook includes

- A Financial Inventory
- Habit tracker
- Debt payoff tracker
- Journaling prompts
- Side hustle brainstorm worksheet
- A daily planner
- And more...

It's not essential for completing the book but it will help you organize everything you're learning and executing. You can download it for free at: modernfrugality.com/debtfreeworkbook

And for a complete list of all the studies, books, and resources I mention in this book, be sure to visit: modernfrugality.com/payoffyourdebtbookresources

DEDICATION

For Travis & Kai,
you brighten my days and drive my work. I love you.

PAY OFF YOUR DEBT FOR GOOD

INTRODUCTION

The idea that it takes 21 days to form a habit is misguided at best.

Even if you practice something every day for 21 days, that's not nearly enough time to go through all the phases that make an action really stick with you.

So why write a 21-day guide to creating a sustainable debt-free journey?

Because it feels attainable. Our minds can grasp a bite-size, finite period of time more easily than a seemingly endless journey with a long list of tasks and more than its fair share of difficulties.

1

And that's essentially what paying off debt is like.

It's difficult, restrictive and feels like it's never going to end. But you probably already know that. There are countless books and courses that will teach you the importance of getting out of debt, making a budget and investing. But they don't prepare you for the day-to-day decisions, temptations, and priorities that conflict with reaching your goal.

I know this because I spent two years absorbing every nugget of financial information I could while my husband and I paid off $78K of debt. Not because I needed to know more, but because choosing to stay committed was nearly impossible some days and I was struggling.

When my husband and I started our journey to paying off our debt, we thought if we worked hard and got lucky, we could be debt free in five years.

We dove headfirst into our goal. We got side jobs, cut our expenses, and once we got going, it wasn't long before what should've taken us five years was over in 23 months.

But along the way, we also lost jobs, were underemployed, spent too much, didn't spend enough, fought with each other, and fought with ourselves. Between the two of us we experienced almost every setback you could imagine.

With everything working against us, it wasn't our budgeting method or side jobs alone that pulled us out of debt quickly. Rules and baby steps didn't cut three years off our timeline. What got us out of debt fast was thinking outside the box we'd been given and making it work for us.

Not only did paving our own way benefit us financially; by the time we finished paying off our debt, I'd also learned things about myself, my partner, our relationship, and what I value that would've taken me decades to learn alone.

So many people say they want to be debt free. They make New Year's resolutions, start new budgets on the first of the month, and commit to getting their spending under control, just to find themselves back to their old habits several weeks later.

If you've ever "fallen off the wagon" or found yourself giving up when things get hard or boring, it's time for you to get back up and pay off your debt for good.

In this book I'm going to walk you through everything I've learned, observed and researched about how to stick to the task of paying off debt and actually finish.

In the years since we've become free from consumer debt, I've had the opportunity to compare what we did with dozens of others who've paid off their debt. I've met and befriended hundreds of debt-free men and women, heard their stories, and learned how their experiences differed from mine.

Becoming debt free isn't complicated, but it is difficult. That's why I'm giving you 21 days of action items not so you can trudge through this journey, but to make it meaningful. The point isn't to do everything over 21 consecutive days, but to spread it out as far as you need to.

You'll get the most out of this book if you read through it once then go back and complete the tasks. By the time you finish, you'll have insight and perspective to make every bump in the road an opportunity for self-improvement.

By the end of this book you'll know:

- Your entire financial picture
- The psychology behind your relationship with money
- How to let go of the unhealthy baggage you associate with money
- How to stay motivated (and how to persevere when you're struggling)
- How to efficiently form habits that will have you finally sticking to a budget
- How to break impulsive spending habits

- The things you value and the things you no longer need to waste money on
- How to simplify and improve your life to serve your new goals and habits

You also have access to a free workbook where you can practice every action step in the book. You can get the download at modernfrugality.com/debtfreeworkbook.

For many people, debt is the chain that holds them back from living life to the fullest. It can prevent you from saving for a home, retiring with dignity, leaving a toxic job, or being able to spend more time with your kids.

Paying off debt isn't the answer to your financial troubles, but it will be the catalyst for doing amazing things with your money. Without the weight of debt, you'll be free to live life the way you want to, not the way your bills tell you to.

When we had debt we were chained to our payments, watching our interest rise as our principal stayed the same. We now have a six-month emergency fund, have paid for an almost-new SUV in cash, and invest 40% of our income. And it's only been two years since we made our final payment.

Even better than that, we were able to take the lessons we learned and the habits we'd formed into other areas of our lives. We give more generously, wake up earlier, and exercise more consistently.

If you're looking for a cut-and-dry guide to paying off debt that tells you exactly what you need to do with no room for deviation...this is not the book for you. But if you've read the plans and are still struggling, keep reading.

Over 21 days you'll set the foundation personally and environmentally to create a lifestyle that supports your debt free journey.

Will it be difficult? Yes.
Will it be like this forever? No.
Will it be worth it in a way you can't even realize right now? Absolutely.

The information in this book has the ability to change your entire life. So if you are sick and tired of never getting anywhere with your debt payoff and you want to learn how to become the person your finances deserve, then get started RIGHT NOW.

DAY 1

FACE YOUR DEBT

In America, we buy things to bring validation, elevation and ease to our lives. We get degrees from colleges we can't afford, cars that cost as much as we make in a year and are willing to pay $119 per year for free shipping.

And if you ask, somehow we're able to justify every purchase. You need a new car for safety, you got a great deal on the dining room set, It's cheaper to wash your clothes at home so might as well spring for the deluxe washer and dryer.

You've made plenty of money mistakes you regret. Some taught you a lesson, others you're trying to forget.

The ones we're trying to get at are the ones you're still rationalizing. The money choices you make that keep you living paycheck-to-paycheck and stuck in a cycle of debt.

That is, if you're anything like me.

After completing grad school I had $50K in debt compounding at 6.6% interest. I wasn't irresponsible: I studied harder than I partied, bought generic brand products, and drove a 15-year old Toyota Camry that I bought for $4K.

On the outside it seemed I was doing everything right. But behind the scenes, I had a stereotypical toxic relationship with money.

My salary was less than $40K per year, and while that should've been more than enough for a single twentysomething to live off, I couldn't make extra payments to my student loans. I spent every dollar that I made because I "deserved it."

Debt comes with a lot of guilt and shame, but you can't fully live in debt freedom if you're carrying around that emotional baggage. You and your debt are separate. You didn't get into debt because you're stupid, bad with money, incapable of self-control, or any of the lies you've told yourself in the past. In fact, it's time to let go of all of those past decisions that got you into debt and focus on now and the future.

You can't change who you were and what you did, but you can become whoever you want and do whatever you want starting right now.

Today's Action Steps:
- Make a list of all your debts.
- Post a chart to mark your progress.
- Write down the part you played in getting to your current financial state.

DAY 2

WHAT'S YOUR WHY?

I avoided my debt for several years. Not because I didn't want to pay it off, but because it scared me more to face it than to get rid of it. It wasn't until I got engaged that I learned my "why," and it wasn't until much later that I identified how important that moment was.

My husband proposed four days after his college graduation, and told me his first priority once we were married was to pay off his student loans. I was a little shocked but mostly disappointed because I did not want to pay mine off, mostly because I had double the amount.

I selfishly argued my case as to why we should not pay off our loans. But then he started to explain all the reasons we should. The things we could do, the money we'd save in interest, and how much more flexible our lives could be if we sacrificed for a few years right now.

At first, I thought he was keeping me from living my best life. Eventually, I realized he was telling me how to fully live my best life.

See, my dream is to grow our family through fostering and adoption. Fostering is hard work, lots of appointments, time, and money goes into it. I expected a stressful life with $600 monthly loan payments and working just to break even. It sounds silly, but I could have never imagined for myself a life of financial freedom and flexibility.

My Why became making my future more flexible so I can better invest in whatever child comes into our home.

Are you dreaming small for yourself? Allow me to dream bigger for you. What would you do if you had no debt, could afford every bill every month, and had enough consistent income to be flexible with your time?

That's your Why. Write it down.

Your Why is your purpose, the reason that drives you to say "no" when you want to say "yes" or turn around when you start heading to the nearest sale. It supports you when you're down and motivates you when you're on a roll.

Simon Sinek, author of the books Start With Why and Find Your Why, tells us that companies who start by explaining why they do what they do are much more successful than companies who only promote what their product does.

The same is true for you. Determining your Why and committing to it is so much more powerful than knowing the benefits and ways to become debt free.

In Find Your Why, Sinek introduces the Why Statement. It's a clear statement for articulating your Why to yourself and others. The format is simple: "To ____ so that ____."

The first blank is your contribution and the second is the impact of your contribution. My Why Statement was "To pay off debt so that I can have schedule flexibility with my kids and fully invest in them."

I'm happy to say that two years after becoming debt free, I had our son and now I get to work from home. I freelance, so I decide how many pieces I want to take on each month. If life happens and I have to push back a deadline, I'm open with my clients about it. I can afford to work less now because of the hard work I did then.

Once our son is a year old, we're going to start the process of becoming licensed foster parents. I'm excited to see this dream become a reality and even more excited to be able to do it with less stress than I once thought was required. I hope that one day, when you experience the fulfillment of your Why, you'll feel the same.

Today's Action Step:

- Write down your Why Statement and put it somewhere you'll see it everyday.

DAY 3

SET YOUR GOALS

Paying off debt is a goal in itself, so why do we have to think about goal setting any further?

Because goal-setting is a powerful psychological tool. Making steps to reach goals triggers our brains to release dopamine, the neurotransmitter that causes us to feel happy and satisfied. Having more goals that can be achieved at regular intervals produces a chemical chain reaction that helps you pay off debt faster.

And the goals you can set on the path to debt freedom are virtually endless. You'll have spending limits to target, earning goals, payment goals, lifestyle challenges to overcome, and even relationship goals. When you break down these processes and make goals around them, you'll find you reach the big goal faster.

To get my spending under control, I would try to "fast" from spending on certain things for weeks at a time. Every day I got closer to meeting my goal, I had more motivation to keep going. There were times every day that I wanted to give up, but with every day those moments got shorter and shorter. And by the end, I was so proud of myself I couldn't wait to take on the next challenge.

While there's no shortage of goals you can set, only focus on one or two at a time. Multitasking makes you less efficient. In Gary Keller's book, The One Thing, he proposes that by focusing on one thing at a time we actually get more done at a faster rate than when we're trying to juggle multiple goals.

Look at your problem areas, timeline, debts, etc. and write down the goals you want to accomplish that will help you pay off your debt faster and choose one or two to start with.

You can do this on the Day 3 worksheet in the free workbook that accompanies this book. Find it at modernfrugality.com/debtfreeworkbook.

The Psychology of Goals

After your brainstorm, work on refining those goals. Because there are ways you can think about and write your goals to help you achieve them. Here are some things to consider:

Setting goals causes a shift in your identity. When you set a goal, your brain starts to associate your identity with the desired outcome. Say you set a goal to stop going to the mall every weekend. Your brain thinks you shouldn't be at the mall and will produce constant tension between reality and the goal. That tension will internally motivate you to do something else on the weekend. And if you do go to the mall, it won't bring you as much enjoyment as it used to.

If your goal is to spend better, start acting and making decisions like someone who makes good spending decisions. Your brain will support the change.

Shorter is better. With every achievement on the path to meeting your goal, your body releases sweet, sweet dopamine into your brain. And you now know that the more hits of dopamine your brain gets, the easier it'll be to stay focused and motivated.

Well, missing a goal has an equal, opposite reaction. The dopamine gets cut off and you'll feel like giving up. So make every effort to avoid that cutoff by breaking your ultimate debt payoff goal into smaller ones.

No goal is too small. Start by making a payment that's more than the minimum balance due, or transferring your emergency fund to an account that's harder to spend. Whatever it is, make the first few goals ridiculously easy so you can get that dopamine train running.

Setting goals fosters resourcefulness. The deadlines, numbers, and parameters associated with goals foster the ability to find quick and clever ways to overcome difficulties. Resourcefulness will force you to redefine what's possible and show you how much more you're capable of doing than you once thought.

People can get very creative when trying to reach their goals, so don't let difficulties derail you. Use them to learn and think outside the box.

Goal-Setting Methods

Goal-setting researchers Gary Latham and Edwin Locke evaluated dozens of their own studies along with those of other scientists to see what kind of goals people followed through on the most. They found that the best goals are those that are specific and difficult, but not outrageously tough.

In order to ensure your goals are as effective as possible, there are several methods you can use to formulate them.

The SMART criteria is the most well-known. It helps you focus on the achievability of your goal.

- Specific: The goal should be clear and simple. You should be able to write it down concisely.
- Measurable: You should be able to easily track your progress.
- Achievable: The goal should be realistically achievable in your time frame.
- Relevant: For the purposes of this book, the goal should play a significant part in getting you closer to paying off your debt.
- Time-bound: The goal should have a deadline to give it a sense of urgency and importance.

People love the SMART criteria because it provides hyper-focused parameters that give tangible feedback on how you're progressing with your goals. But strict criteria don't work for everyone. If you want an acronym that's simpler but just as effective, try ABC.

- Achievable/Aim-High: The goal should be challenging, but achievable.
- Believable: Believe in yourself and your capacity to move closer to paying off debt.
- Committed: Commit to work on the goal on a daily basis.

The ABC method focuses more on the challenging aspect of the goal, which can help be a catalyst for meeting bigger goals faster. You should still be able to clearly write down your goal, but there's more flexibility. The drawback is that you have to have the resiliency to be OK if—and when—you occasionally fall short.

For either method, here are some tips for achieving your goals:

Write them down. George Wu, a professor of behavioral science, encouraged marathon runners to write down their finishing goal for an upcoming race. Most of them already had a goal in mind, but Wu found that the ones who actually wrote down their goals ended up running faster than the control group who did not. Just like the runners, you'll go faster by making your goals tangible.

Find "fresh start" moments. The first day of the year, month, or week are naturally "fresh start" moments that can make your goals more measurable. You can also choose special dates like a birthday or anniversary. The mistake you don't want to make in choosing your "fresh start" is to use it as an excuse to put off starting a goal. Make them meaningful but make them soon.

Share your goals. Don't just write down your goals for you to see. Share them with others, too. A great place to do this is on Instagram. Use hashtags like #debtfreejourney and #debtfreecommunity on your posts to connect with a large community of people paying off debt and be a part of their progress too.

Today's Action Step:

- Think about and write down your first few goals using the method of your choice.

DAY 4

TAKE INVENTORY

People who succeed in the long run know every aspect of their finances. From income and expenses to insurance policies and wills, you need to know everything that could affect your debt payoff.

This isn't just knowing for knowing's sake. Taking a financial inventory will eliminate surprises that could derail the momentum you're going to build and give you peace of mind to make smarter decisions.

You probably already have your income and expenses written down, but there's a lot more to cover, even in the simplest financial inventory. A comprehensive financial inventory includes:

- Debts and liabilities
- Income
- Expenses
- Assets and insurance
- Important documents
- Contacts and login credentials

The first three — debt, income, and expenses — are most relevant to becoming debt free, and where we'll spend most of our time in this book. Everything else will give you a clearer picture of what's beyond debt freedom and prepare you for a smooth transition into it.

Everything you need to inventory is on the Day 4 worksheet in your free workbook at modernfrugality.com/debtfreeworkbook.

Your Financial Inventory Checklist

It's important to note that this is an inventory, not a to-do list. Don't worry about having everything on it or getting so distracted by it you avoid your debt. You'll have more than enough time to complete it, so don't feel stressed if you need to skip something.

Debts and Liabilities

You compiled a list of your debts on Day 1 and made a visual representation of them. Today you'll add that information to your checklist. Possible debts include:

- Student loans
- Car loans
- Credit card balances
- Personal loans
- Payday loans
- Lines of credit
- Loans from friends and family
- Payments on phones and laptops
- Medical bills

- Mortgage

Don't worry about the order right now, we'll decide that a little later. For now, just get them all written down.

Income

Income obviously plays a crucial role in your debt payoff plan, with the bulk of it coming from your primary salary. But my favorite way to spend less money is to spend more time making it. Side hustles can be an easy way to make money fast, even if they're not extremely lucrative.

You may not have a lot of time, but I promise there's always something you can do to make more money, even in your current full-time job. So in addition to recording what your current income is, this will also serve as a baseline you can challenge yourself to improve.

The income streams to include are:

- Primary salary/ hourly wages

- Freelance work
- Side hustles
- Royalties
- Business income
- Rental income
- Investment income
- Alimony, child support, or other assistance

Write the amount you get monthly from each. For irregular income streams, write down your average monthly earnings.

Expenses

I classify expenses into two categories: fixed and discretionary. Fixed expenses are payments you can't eliminate:

- Basic groceries
- A roof over your head (rent, mortgage, utilities, etc.)
- Anything you need to make money (transportation, uniforms, internet, etc.)

Discretionary expenses are everything else. The goal in adding this to the financial checklist isn't to shame yourself or eliminate your discretionary expenses. It's to write them down and find out where your money is going.

When you can identify the 5-10 places you're spending the most money, you can work to change a few bigger expenses instead of a bunch of little ones. Go as far back as your online banking system will allow (usually 90 days) and list transactions that you see every month.

The easiest way to do this is to export your transactions from your online banking account and upload them in an Excel spreadsheet — or Google Sheets if you don't have Excel. You can then alphabetize the sheet to see how often and how much you're spending everywhere.

And don't forget about annual and semi-annual expenses like registration fees, scheduled car maintenance, and insurance payments. For these, break the total cost down into 12 increments and transfer that amount out of your spending account and into a savings account every month so you can cover it when the bill comes around.

Assets and Insurance

An asset is anything you own that builds your net worth. When your assets equate to more than your debt, you have a positive net worth. Assets you might have include:

- Emergency fund
- Bank accounts
- Retirement accounts
- Education savings accounts
- Health savings accounts
- Brokerage and investment accounts
- Real estate (including your primary home)

Besides your bank account, try to leave these accounts alone. Some people consider taking money out of retirement accounts to pay off debt, especially if it's high-interest credit card debt. But after taxes and the 10% early withdrawal penalty, it's typically not a good financial decision to cash out an investment account early.

You should also find out what types of insurance policies you have. Insurance can sometimes feel like a luxury you can't afford. Unfortunately some insurances can be the difference between an annoying bill and total bankruptcy. Types of insurance to include are:

- Health insurance
- Auto insurance
- Homeowners/renters insurance
- Term life insurance
- Long-term disability insurance
- Whole life or cash-value life insurance
- Long-term care insurance

Be sure to note which policies you have, possible payouts, deductibles, co-insurance, and out-of-pocket maximums, especially with your health insurance. Later on, the deductibles will help you determine how much to save in your emergency fund.

While some of these policies are essential, others aren't. When I did my first financial checklist, I found out that my deceased grandmother had a whole-life insurance policy on me. Since I'm young and healthy, I made the decision to get a term policy and was able to put the cash value of the other policy toward debt.

Do your research and if you have specific questions, talk to unbiased experts in those fields to determine if your particular assets or insurances are worth keeping or better used to eliminate your debt faster.

Also important to note: If you're someone who's considering bankruptcy, this list may be a sobering reality for what you potentially stand to lose. Only in very rare cases is bankruptcy the solution to a debt problem, and in those cases you should be ready for other financial problems to persist long after the bankruptcy discharge.

Important Documents

Often overlooked but just as important as a retirement account or an emergency fund are financial documents. These include:

- Wills
- Power of attorney documents
- Tax documents
- Titles and deeds
- Insurance policy documents
- Passwords and login credentials for financial accounts
- Contacts list for tax and financial professionals

It's important to have copies of all your important documents in a safe and easy-to-access place in case of emergency. The last thing you want to do when you're stressed is tear your house apart looking for a document.

The two most underrated documents on the list are your will and power of attorney documents. If you have assets, you need to make a will. Even if you don't think they're significant, the earlier you decide where everything goes, the more you'll thank yourself in the future.

A power of attorney document allows you to appoint a person to handle your affairs should you become unable to do so. This isn't just for you; you should start talking to your parents about who they want to appoint as their power of attorney as well.

Cameron Huddleston, author of the book Mom and Dad, We Need to Talk, had no reason to think about power of attorney until her mother was diagnosed with dementia. By the time she was diagnosed, it was almost too late for her to be considered cognizant enough to even sign one.

Without it, Cameron would've had to spend thousands of dollars in court fees, fighting to prove she was acting in her mom's best interest any time there was a decision to be made. Cameron was lucky enough to get one just in time.

The last thing you want to do after an accident or diagnosis is fight with lawyers and the medical system. Talk to your loved ones and get the documents you need to make life easier.

Today's Action Steps:

- Fill out your Financial Inventory Checklist.
- Make a note of the missing pieces and get started filling them in.

DAY 5

LET GO

Facing your debt and the rest of your finances can be an emotional roller coaster.

The way you earn, save, and spend money is a result of your history and experiences with it. And for most of us, that history is tainted by guilt and shame for the mistakes we've made or ones that were made for us.

My first job out of college paid $10 an hour. It was a job in my field, using my master's degree. I went home every day and looked at the $50K of student loans I owed and felt hopeless. Soon it started to give me anxiety, and I stopped looking.

I felt so stupid for taking out so much debt. Eventually I gave up trying to pay them off and lowered my payments to $30 a month.

For two years I made $30 monthly payments. I got a better job, better car, moved out of my mom's house, and went out with friends most weekends. The whole time I carried the guilt and shame of thinking "I shouldn't be buying [insert anything here], I should be paying off my student loans."

But I, like most millennials, ignored it, and let it fester to the point where having student loans was normal. Everyone else had them, so I could too. I believed the lie that "I've been like everyone else my whole life and I've gotten by just fine, so it's good enough for my future too."

The guilt and shame came up again once I started paying off my debt. I felt guilty about every purchase, even if it was in the budget. Everytime I messed up I felt shameful, like I wasn't capable of doing it.

I learned it's easy to try to stay normal. It's hard to become someone you don't know how to be.

Paying off debt takes courage like you wouldn't believe. You'll be different, you'll be doing things that are different, and not everyone in your life will be OK with it.

So it's essential that you're mentally strong going into it. And that means letting go of the guilt and shame that are inherently wrapped up in your money mindset.

Letting Go of Guilt

Guilt is the feeling of having done wrong or made a mistake. A healthy relationship with guilt is actually good—it allows us to have empathy for others. An unhealthy level of guilt can cause an unrelenting amount of pain.

Anyone who's ever had money has made a financial mistake. Maybe it's small like a habit of impulse spending, or putting all your appliance purchases on payments. Maybe it's something bigger like being trapped in a cycle of payday loans or buying more house than you can afford.

That's why the first task in this book was to separate yourself from your debt. We can often feel like our debt rules how we identify ourselves in regards to money. But you are not your debt, you don't have to be the person who took on that debt. Stop rationalizing your actions, take responsibility, and forgive yourself.

I wish it were as easy as telling you to stop feeling the negative consequences of guilt and use it to grow, but it's not. So here are some ways you can come to terms with it.

1. Write down one of your financial mistakes and what was going on in your life when you made it. Include how you felt about yourself and others involved. Analyze what your needs were at the time, if they were being met, and if not, why?

2. Identify the catalyst for your behavior. Were you going to college? Going through a divorce? Dealing with low self-esteem?

3. Evaluate how you're judging yourself. Are you comparing yourself or seeking approval from successful family members or wealthy friends? What standards do you want to use to judge yourself?

4. Is there information you have now that you didn't have then? What do you wish you'd known then?

5. What did you learn from the experience, including the aftermath, and how would you handle it differently today?

I did this when coming to terms with my student loans. I felt great when I signed for them! I needed a graduate degree to do what I loved, and in my arrogance I did no research and decided to get my degree no matter the cost.

I didn't fully understand compound interest, and I can't help but hate the guidance counselor who let 19-year-old me sign for so much money without explaining it. I also didn't know there wouldn't be many jobs in my field when I graduated. But I forgave myself for not doing enough research or having information that wasn't available to me. And now, I don't regret taking out those loans in the slightest.

They got me to where I needed to be and helped bring me to where I am today. I wouldn't have half of the great things in my life today without those student loans. I'm proud of myself today, but it took time, hard work, and a lot of introspection to get there. And now, not only have I learned from my financial mistakes; I'm also able to empathize with others who've made the same ones.

Every mistake we make is an opportunity to one day help someone else avoid or work through the same mistake.

Even if it feels silly and awkward, share your experience and what you're learning. It's an opportunity to set you on a path to growth that you wouldn't have started otherwise. And don't let feelings of guilt persuade you into feeling sorry for yourself. You are exactly where you were meant to be right now and as long as you stay committed, you have the opportunity to grow exponentially through this debt-free journey.

Letting Go of Shame

Shame is different from guilt. Shame is a painful feeling of inadequacy. Or as famed researcher Dr. Brene Brown puts it:

Guilt is "I made a mistake."
Shame is "I am a mistake."

While guilt can be healthy if it teaches you a lesson and helps you empathize with others, there is no healthy level of shame. Shame leads to feeling trapped, isolated, and powerless.

In her research, Dr. Brown has found that there are four elements to building resilience to shame:

1. Recognize shame and its physical (heart racing, chest tightness, etc.) triggers. We often feel shame physically before we realize it mentally.

2. Recognize the external factors that led to your feeling of shame. See the link between what you're feeling and society's often-conflicting and shaming expectations.

3. Connect with others to receive and offer empathy. Do the hard task of reaching out for support.

4. Discuss and deconstruct the feelings of shame. Separate shame from other emotions.

Identify the people in your life who make you feel like you're not skilled enough to accomplish this or you don't deserve to succeed. Recognize how they make you feel and talk about it with others. Don't keep shame in the dark.

We're conditioned to think we have to do everything and do it perfectly so we don't look weak. But there's no way to be successful on that mission. You will mess up, life will ruin your plan, but the beautiful thing about life is that you can revise the plan and move on.

If you're feeling shame about your financial situation, or any part of your life, don't sweep it under the rug or try to get by on your might. Build resilience to shame so you can get through the tough times even when you're not feeling 100%.

Dealing With Anxiety and Depression While Paying Off Debt

Sometimes the difficulty we face persevering through our debt payoff stems from a deeper issue than just mindset. Debt makes people more susceptible to anxiety and depression, and the journey is even harder for those who struggle with it regularly.

Anxiety and depression are more than the result of a simple chemical imbalance. Recent studies have found it's a complex combination of stress, medication, life events, brain structure, and neurotransmitters that have stopped working together properly.

And few things are more stressful than financial problems and expensive life events.

If you're dealing with your guilt and shame but still feel like you're not making any emotional progress, get outside help.

Talk to a professional. Whether it's a licensed counselor or someone with experience dealing with these thoughts and emotions, talk to someone who can help. You'll be surprised at how cathartic it is to talk and what a little outside perspective can do for you.

Try medication or supplements. If you've tried talking but still can't shake the feelings, there's no shame in seeking help through medication, CBD oil, or other recommendations from your doctor.

Get moving. According to a Harvard study, both low and high-intensity exercise sustained over time can help relieve depression. Exercise releases feel-good chemicals and proteins that cause nerve cell growth in the part of the brain that regulates mood.

Debt is never bad enough for you to be better off alone or dead. Your spouse does not need to be free from you and your debt, your family would not be better off with your life insurance money, and there is nothing you're going through that hasn't been overcome by someone else before you.

There is always a way out that doesn't involve harming yourself or your relationships. Be willing to seek help when you need it.

Today's Action Steps:
- Answer the guilt and shame questions in your workbook.
- Give yourself permission to let go: Write down the feelings that aren't helping you be better, then rip them up and throw them in the fire (or the trash can).

DAY 6

FIND ACCOUNTABILITY

I want to start the conversation on accountability with the unavoidable fact that it is easier to pay off debt with two incomes versus one. That proves to be a big barrier for my single friends to achieving debt freedom. But too many people use their singleness as an excuse as to why they shouldn't even try. I know because it was my excuse.

Living on a single income is hard enough, but it's even harder to try to get ahead on one. What's not true is the idea that debt freedom can't happen for you because of your single income.

I have single people tell me that the personal finance advice they hear can't apply to them because of their singleness. That they still have to pay the full amount of things couples split like rent, utilities, Netflix, etc.

It might be harder and you may have to get more creative than your dual-income friends, but you can pay off debt on a single income. I've been following debt payoff stories long enough to know plenty of single people who've become debt free, even single parents and single-income families.

For the single person, one thing more important than the number of income streams you currently have is accountability. Dual income or single, when trying to change our habits or accomplish a goal, we all need someone there cheering us on and nudging us back in the right direction when we get off track.

And just like deciding to make better financial choices isn't a one-time thing, neither is the accountability needed to make those decisions.

An accountability partner is a relationship centered around helping two people reach a goal and celebrate success. It's not just someone who you call when you're about to swipe your card at Kohl's. Your partner is your place to celebrate victories and vent struggles and frustrations.

The relationship goes both ways. You'll also help and celebrate your partner. Sometimes I need to hear myself help someone through something for those same words to sink into my head.

To have a successful accountability relationship there are a few things you'll need:

Know what you need to be held accountable for and define specific outcomes for it. Do you have an overspending habit at Target or on the latest tech gadgets? Do you beat yourself up for spending money? Know your triggers and be specific when sharing them.

Make accountability a priority. Accountability starts with you. If you schedule time to talk or say you'll check in with a certain frequency, honor the commitment and show up. You have to be committed to the process if you're going to succeed.

Establish a tracking system that works for you. If you're paying off debt, you can track more than payment increments. Track the percentage by which your spending goes down and your income goes up or anything else that gets you closer to debt freedom.

Choose your partner wisely. Don't pick a friend who'll help you rationalize your takeout order or one who will shame you for any wrong decision. Be thoughtful with whom you choose. One of my favorite African proverbs says, "If you want to go fast, go alone. If you want to go far, go together."

Where to Find Your Accountability Partner

Finding a good accountability partner is probably easier than you think. You just have to know where to look and how to approach them.

Start at Home

When you're married or sharing finances with a partner, then you have a live-in accountability partner. Having your spouse as accountability is a blessing and a curse. You're each more invested in the other's success, but you're also more judgemental and afraid to share failure.

I love coffee. There was a time that I'd stop at Starbucks any time I passed one, unless I already had a drink in my hand. For some reason this really peeved my husband. I got a lot of judgement and it even spurred a few fights between us.

Thankfully I brew most of my coffee at home now, and after a decade I am proud to say I am no longer a Starbucks Gold member. But we had to have some conversations about separating our accountability relationship from our personal one.

If you're going to be accountability partners with your spouse, agree to be completely honest and have compassion for each other. Emotions and expectations are higher in this relationship, so run your interactions through the filter of whether you'd say the same thing to a friend first.

Unfortunately, your spouse may not come around to the idea of debt freedom at the same time as you, and we'll talk about this more later. For now, don't force them to be on this journey if they're not ready. They'll listen to what you say, but they'll remember what you do. Keep setting an example and showing them the fruits of your labor and eventually they'll come around.

Ask a Friend

If you don't have a spouse or partner, or yours isn't on board with debt freedom, you'll have to look outside the house.

When choosing a friend as an accountability partner, you probably won't pick your best friend. Observe the people in your life and follow a few guidelines to create a partnership that will thrive.

Find someone with discipline. Look for characteristics of discipline in your friends. They wake up early, can maintain a workout routine or regimen, they're a self starter, etc. No one's perfect but if you see a few of these signs you've probably found a disciplined person.

Choose someone you won't want to disappoint. This is why your best friend may not be your accountability partner. You know they'll love you no matter how many times you mess up. So pick someone who's not so invested in your life, but more so in your success.

Find someone who has time to invest. You might have the right person in mind, but if they have too much going on to be your partner, it won't work.

Find someone who's also willing to be held accountable. It's just as productive to help someone as it is to be helped. Make sure the person you choose also has something they want accountability for.

Never stop looking. Your partnership may not be picture perfect, especially the first time you try this thing. Things change, life happens, and even a really great partnership may have to end. So never stop looking for accountability partners—the more the merrier! That way if one partnership dissolves, you'll have another to fall back on.

As you practice this new kind of relationship, be ready to show a new kind of vulnerability. You should exhibit all the qualities you're looking for in an accountability partner.

Go to Social Media

When everyone in your life is still content to brunch their paycheck away, there's a community of people on social media to turn to.

On Instagram you can search the hashtag #debtfreecommunity to find over 600K posts from people side-hustling, spending less, and paying off debt. Spend some time interacting with people in the community and you might find an accountability partner there.

There are also groups on Facebook for all kinds of people paying off debt, pursuing financial independence, and being better spenders. Our group, Frugal Friends Community, is a great one for frugal tips and supportive friends.

You'll never regret having an accountability partner, even if just for a season, while you're trying to change your habits and redesign your financial life. So take the chance and get one.

Today's Action Step:

• Start your search for an accountability partner.

DAY 7

CREATE A SIMPLE SPENDING SYSTEM

This would be the point in the personal finance book where the author tells you to make a budget. And I will, but let me be honest:

I hate budgets.

After making several dozen while paying off our debt, I was never able to stick to ANY. Which is sad, because I'm the one who made them. It was a huge discouragement even when we were making good progress on our debt.

With all the personal finance advice out there, I asked people why they still struggled to maintain a budget. I got answers like:

"Sticking to it is difficult."
"I don't want to do it."
"I've got a really small income and it gets frustrating."

All the answers shared the same themes: fear, laziness, and life getting in the way. So it seems we should be talking more about those things than whether you should set aside $50 or $100 in your grocery budget.

You can fix fear and laziness—and we will talk about those—but you can't fix life. It's always going to throw you something that will mess up your budget. Oh, and when life is going well, those fear and laziness habits tend to creep up again.

Budgeting is restrictive, guilt-inducing, and not sustainable. But, while budgets may be the bane of my existence, the sad fact is that you need one.

I may not have stuck the landing on any of my budgets, but the process of making them helped me get a grasp on our spending and income. We were able to get on the same page with our priorities, keep an eye on our income and expenses, and have tough money conversations we wouldn't have had otherwise. For those reasons, I love budgets.

Do you know what a budget offers, behind all the restrictions? Freedom. Freedom to spend money with intention; mental freedom that comes with knowing you can pay your bills; and freedom to change it up to work for you.

Because of my love/hate relationship with budgeting, I needed something new that would work for me in the long term. I needed a system that combined the awareness and guidance of a budget with the flexibility and sustainability that not having one offers.

Now, instead of budgeting, I have a Simple Spending System.

Every month I make our Simple Spending System in three steps:

1. Record Income from last month.
2. Pay all my bills and make any other financial contributions as soon as possible.
3. Spend whatever's left on things I value.

That's it. It's the most sustainable form of budgeting out there and it's probably the one your favorite personal finance personality is actually doing while they're telling you how important it is to allocate every dollar.

But I didn't get to this point overnight, and neither will you. It was after making all those budgets that "spent" every dollar that I learned what my weaknesses were and how I value spending money. Once I learned myself and put my finances on autopilot, the Simple Spending System started to work.

Going from mindless spender to conscious non-budgeter takes months—sometimes years—and I probably have enough insight to write an entire follow-up book on the process. Since this is a book about paying off debt, not budgeting, for now I'll include only what you need to know to get started.

1. Spend Every Dollar

You thought you were going to get off easy didn't you? Before you can graduate, you've got to go to school for your budget. But this won't be hard because you have everything you need in your financial inventory.

Go through your list of transactions for the last 90 days, write a budget reflective of those values and "spend" every dollar of your predicted monthly income on it.

You don't need to use a pretty premade budget template with generic categories and suggested amounts. Write down the things you actually bought and how much you actually spent. Be specific with your categories. If you have a habit of going to three different grocery stores every week, don't make a "groceries" category. Start with "Walmart", "Trader Joe's", and

"Kroger" categories. Specific categories will help you identify your strengths and weaknesses faster.

For instance, clothing is a common line item on budget spreadsheets. I'm not a big fashionista, but because it was there I'd put $10-$20 in it every month. After a few months I realized I was going $10-$20 over budget in coffee shops every month, but I hadn't bought a single item of clothing.

It seems silly, but I didn't realize that until I started tracking it. Making an overly detailed budget isn't sustainable, but it is helpful when you're starting out.

You can find a blank budget template in the free workbook available with this book at modernfrugality.com/debtfreeworkbook.

2. Go 10%

Now that you have a detailed budget with lots of categories and you've assigned every dollar of your income to each, it's time to start pruning.

In the areas you want to decrease your spending, shave 10% off the value you spent last month. If you want to increase your income, shoot for a 10% increase in a side hustle — which could be any amount if you haven't started one yet!

It's tempting to look at your $300 spending at Chipotle and want to change that to $50 next month. But your habits are deeply ingrained, and while you may succeed at that $50 budget for one month, it's highly likely you'll only make it two or three months with that drastic of a change. Habits are changed in small doses, so go slowly.

3. Prioritize

Now spend time prioritizing. First you'll prioritize your bills. It's the 21st century, so you should have everything on autopay.

Louder for the people in the back: YOU SHOULD BE AUTOMATING EVERYTHING.

If you can, schedule as many as possible to be drafted at the beginning of the month or as soon as you get paid.

Next, prioritize your saving and debt payoff goals. The first of these is an emergency fund, which we'll talk about soon. Next is paying off your debt. You should try to focus on one goal at a time, that doesn't mean you won't have smaller saving goals come up — like saving for a family reunion or replacing an old car — while you pay off debt. But don't let two big goals compete for your attention. No matter how important each one is, it ultimately slows down both.

After you've afforded the most important things, spend on what you value. The reason you start with a cumbersome lengthy budget is to learn what spending is habitual and what is valuable. When I was going $10-$20 over budget on coffee, I felt guilty every time, even though I was technically under budget from not spending the "clothing" money.

You'll spend a few months shaving money off your budget categories and paying attention to where you're mindlessly spending before you see patterns, so start to be on the lookout for them.

4. Simplify Your Spending System

Once you've automated your finances, learned the places you overspend, changed your habits, and feel confident in the places you are spending, you'll naturally simplify your complex budget into a manageable spending system.

I look at our income from the previous month, subtract my monthly bills and investment contributions, and spend the rest. I use an app to track my spending and when I get close to the limit (which I rarely do now), I'll leave my credit card at home.

Sometimes I'll have a medical bill or other large payment that I can't cover with one month's income. Now I have a separate fund for that, but when we were paying off debt I would've used my emergency fund.

Your budget is simply a way to gain control of your spending. Budget in a way that allows you to fall in love with the way you spend and you'll find it easy to stick to your budget.

Today's Action Steps:

- Make your exhaustive budget.
- Identify your spending habits, choose one and make a 10% change.

DAY 8

START AN EMERGENCY FUND

Right now you may be revved up to dive right into paying off debt, throwing all your extra income and savings toward it because you want it gone.

Alternatively, you might have a couple grand sitting in savings that you can't bear to let go of while you keep putting things on credit.

Neither of those methods are sustainable for getting you out of debt.

In order to get out of debt, you need to stop going into debt. And when surprise expenses come up you need to be prepared to pay for them without relying on money that's not yours. You also need to be intentional with how much you save instead of hoarding money out of fear.

An emergency fund is the solution. It's money set aside for expenses you can't schedule. Things like a roof repair after your neighbor's tree falls on your roof, a car wreck that leaves you unable to work for a few weeks, or an illness that requires prescriptions not covered by insurance.

There are a lot of things we try to rationalize as emergencies that really aren't. A surprise sale on bike shorts isn't an emergency, even if you're training for the Tour de France. A sale on Instant Pots isn't an emergency even if you're cooking at home more.

Most medical bills give you about 90 days before your account goes into collections, so for smaller bills you have time to change your spending or work overtime to afford it. The prescription and copay that are due up front are a different story. You don't have time to make more money to cover those. That's what the emergency fund is for.

There are two stages of an emergency fund: starter and full.

How Much Should You Have in Your Starter Emergency Fund?

Your starter emergency fund may be the most practical element of your debt payoff journey. If you go in, guns blazing, to pay off your debt, life will happen and there'll be a situation that requires money you don't have.

Without an emergency fund, that situation becomes a crisis where decisions are made under stress, more debt is accumulated, and discouragement erodes the mental progress you've made. With an emergency fund, that situation is an inconvenient blip on the radar.

The amount you have in your starter emergency fund is up to you. $1000 is a safe number to start with. If you're young and have financial support from parents, then

$500 is probably enough. If you're a single-income family with four kids, you may want to save the amount of your health insurance deductible, or more.

You can use your financial inventory to see your insurance deductibles and understand your coverage to determine your starter fund. Base the size of your starter emergency fund on your job volatility and risk for emergencies, not your income.

Whatever number you choose, build it fast. This is a great time to sell some furniture on Facebook Marketplace, work overtime, or cut out restaurant spending for a few weeks. The quicker you get your starter fund established, the faster you can start working on your debt.

Why You Shouldn't Have a Full Emergency Fund (Yet)

You may actually already have your emergency fund saved. That was me. I was single, had $7,000 sitting in my savings account, and still got stressed about making full payments on my student loan.

There was virtually no way I was going to have an emergency that would cost me $7,000 up front. Sure, I could've had an accident with bills that would total $7,000, but those would trickle out over a few months —plenty of time to pay off with a smaller emergency fund and some creative saving hacks—especially when I worked up to making large payments on my debt.

If you're the kind of person who swears they need a full emergency fund before paying off debt, you don't. But you also don't need to drain your account to $1000. Think about the past several years and tally up all the big emergencies you've had. What did they cost? How close together were they? How many have charged you up front?

Chances are, the amount you need in your emergency fund during your debt payoff is far less than what you're carrying. If you can't bring yourself to clear it out in one fell swoop, make transfers over the next six months to bring your fund down to the appropriate size. That length of time will show you that you don't have to live in fear of the what-ifs because you're preparing for them differently now.

On the bright side, the pressure to refill your full emergency fund will motivate you to pay off debt even faster. So there's an extra incentive!

Where to Put Your Emergency Fund

Keep your emergency fund in a place that's easily accessible but not immediately accessible. Put a barrier between you and that chunk of cash. The easiest way to do that is by opening a high-interest savings account at an online bank.

Online banks have been gaining popularity in the last 10 years for waiving fees big banks love to charge and offering interest payments they can't compete with. I've transferred most of my banking to these online banks, keeping one local account for when I need to do business in person.

Bankrate monitors high-yield savings accounts and keeps an updated list of the highest yielding ones each month. When choosing one, make sure you can transfer money to outside accounts free of charge, and that they offer a checking account with a debit card and a mobile banking app.

You want to be able to easily transfer the money from your emergency fund out of savings to whatever checking account you want to use to pay for your emergency. We have ours in a savings account that has its own debit card so we don't need to transfer anything.

I don't carry the debit card for our emergency fund, so if there's an emergency, I'd have to go home and get it. In the very rare case I'd need to use it and can't go home first, I'd pay for it from my day-to-day checking account and transfer my emergency fund money over through the mobile app or when I get home. It takes three days to get there, so it would have to be a life-threatening emergency for me to do it that way.

Don't invest your emergency fund. It sounds like a good idea but an investment account doesn't have a debit card and withdrawing from it is more difficult than a savings account.

Certificates of deposit (CDs), while offering interest rates higher than savings accounts, are even harder to access than investment accounts if you need to before the term is up. So play it safe and go with a high-yield savings account.

What to Do After You Use Your Emergency Fund

When you have an emergency, you'll need to put your debt payoff on hold until you replenish your emergency fund. That could mean you're back in the game next month, or it could mean waiting a few months due to a job loss or baby on the way.

Be mentally prepared for this. Emergencies are the number-one thing that end a healthy debt-free journey. It's so easy once you lose momentum to not get back on the train at all. Commit to maintaining the same momentum getting back on track as you had before the emergency and you'll see very little delay in the time it takes you to become debt free.

Today's Action Steps:

- Open a high-yield savings account at an online bank where you don't do your day-to-day banking.
- Decide what amount your starter emergency fund will be.
- Start funding it.
- If you're already at your target amount, stop funding it.

DAY 9

STRATEGIZE YOUR DEBT PAYOFF

We talked about goals earlier and that you should have a lot of smaller ones but they should all be moving you toward the big goal of paying off debt. That's because having one goal eliminates "goal competition."

Psychologists say the greatest barrier to achieving your goals is the other goals you have, so by having multiple big goals like trying to pay off debt, save for a house, and lose weight all at the same time, you lower your chances of meeting any of them.

So strategize your debt payoff in a way that makes it easy for you to create those smaller goals that get you to debt freedom faster. Most people use either the debt snowball or debt avalanche methods to do this.

Debt Snowball Method

If you're familiar with Dave Ramsey, then you've heard of the debt snowball.

You list all your debts from smallest to largest and pay the minimum on everything except the smallest. Put all your effort toward the smallest debt until it's paid off then add the money you would've paid toward that debt toward what you're paying on the next smallest debt. You keep doing that until every debt is paid off.

The benefit of the debt snowball is the quick win you get from paying off that first debt completely. The gripe everyone has about it is the extra money you pay in interest by not prioritizing the highest-interest debts first.

If you think about it, loans are supposed to work in favor of the debt snowball. Credit card interest rates are high because you're "supposed to" keep the balance low enough to pay it off every month. Mortgage interest rates are typically low because that loan stays with you longer.

Ramsey says psychology is the real reason people don't finish paying off debt and the speed that the snowball method promotes will negate any advantage an interest-first method saves you. I agree with him on this, but that doesn't mean you should write off the debt avalanche.

Debt Avalanche Method

The debt avalanche method is loved by math nerds because it's the same concept as the debt snowball. But instead of starting with the smallest debt, you tackle the debt with the highest interest rate first and follow the interest rates in order until you're debt free.

You can't go wrong with either. Both methods focus on one debt at a time to eliminate that goal competition that holds you back.

Personally, I used a combination of the two. When I started, I had a $4K car loan at 3% interest, $50K student loan at 6.55%, and my husband's $24K student loan with multiple rates that averaged around 4%.

I paid off my car first to get that quick win even though the interest rate was low. Then we paid off my student loan because the interest rate was double what some of my husband's rates were, and then we finished with his loan.

Design and follow the method that works for you. As long as it's based on singular goals that build on each other versus compete with one another, it'll serve you in becoming debt free.

Strategies to Avoid

The debt snowball and debt avalanche both make debt payoff more manageable, but there's no getting around the fact that they're both difficult.

That's why people believe taking out a low-interest loan to pay off higher interest debt is a good way to jumpstart their debt payoff. The math might work out, but the reality is that debt consolidation, 401(k) loans, and home equity loans rarely help you become debt free faster or cheaper.

These strategies give the illusion that you've done something when all you've done is move money from one creditor to another. The time you spend applying for these loans and paying off the others is time you could've spent making money for an extra debt payment.

What usually happens is people consolidate their debt then take a break, wasting some or all the savings they just worked for. Worst case scenario: They forget their "Why" altogether and accrue more debt and interest payments. The moral of the story is that if you want to pay off your debt fast, don't look for the easy way out. Do the hard things fast to see the results you want.

Today's Action Steps:

- Choose your debt payoff strategy.
- Make your first extra debt payment (once your starter emergency fund is funded).

DAY 10

GET MOTIVATED, THE RIGHT WAY

Every big life change starts with hope, inspiration, and a little desperation, and ends with the formation of new and improved habits. And the bridge from hope to habit is motivation.

Motivation is defined as the reason a person has for acting in a particular way. It's a common misconception that motivation is what causes us to start behaving in a certain way, but in reality, motivation is what keeps us going.

My motivation to get out of bed in the morning is the cup of coffee waiting for me in the kitchen. Coffee isn't

86

why I started getting out of bed every morning, but it's what keeps me doing it, among other things.

Once you've got your emergency fund secured, you have a budget you can live with, and you're making some headway paying off debt, the hope and inspiration that got you started won't keep you going. That's why you need to develop healthy motivation tactics.

Sometimes it's going to be really easy to find motivation, other times you're burnt out and not even that cup of coffee is enough to get you out of bed. So while filling up your motivation tank is important, you also have to learn how to persevere when it's empty.

The Right Kind of Motivation

Habits expert James Clear says, "Every choice has a price, but when we are motivated, it is easier to bear the inconvenience of action than the pain of remaining the same." Your debt will get — or has already gotten — to the point where the idea of working multiple side hustles and eating at home is more bearable than going another day ignoring your debt.

To adopt the right kinds of motivation for you, first you have to know what healthy motivations do not look like.

Fear is not motivation. Believing that if you don't pay off your debt you'll be broke and sad is not motivation. Fear comes from a scarcity mindset and giving up that mindset is like letting go of the guilt and shame around money. It's hard but it's necessary to live the "free" part of your debt free life.

Knowledge is not motivation. You can't get to debt-free by knowing everything there is to know about personal finance. If you could, you'd probably already be debt-free. Unfortunately, too many smart people bail on paying off their debt not because they can't figure out how to do it but because they mistake intelligence for motivation.

Instead, here are the types of motivation you should be looking for:

Extrinsic

Extrinsic motivation is behavior that's driven by external rewards such as money, fame, or praise. More money is an extrinsic motivator for working a side hustle or taking extra hours at work. Avoiding deviation from your grocery list is extrinsic motivation for the external reward of getting a high- five from your husband or wife when you get home.

Choose a reward system that doesn't originate from you. Whether it's a meal at your favorite restaurant, a massage, or getting to put extra money in your travel fund, find healthy external rewards for your accomplishments that don't compete with the bigger goal.

Habitual eating out was hard for me to control, so for my small reward, if I avoided eating at quick-service restaurants all month, I got to eat at my favorite sit-down restaurant. This cost a little extra money, but since my problem wasn't with sit-down restaurants, it was a good motivator and actually saved me money.

For our big reward, I dreamed of going on a cruise. The closer we got to becoming debt free, the more I thought about that cruise and the more I was motivated to be disciplined.

Intrinsic

Intrinsic motivation is your internal drive for success, or sense of purpose. It's doing something because it's personally rewarding or you simply enjoy it. It's the satisfaction of knowing you saved $30 by staying home or the delight of seeing your credit card balance go down after an extra payment.

Take a moment to think about what your intrinsic motivators are. What are the unique things that bring you joy and satisfaction on this journey?

Paying off debt shouldn't feel soul-sucking. There are so many ways to do it. You have to choose the methods that reward your soul. If couponing brings you joy and you don't like Aldi, then keep clipping. And don't feel guilty sacrificing a higher-paying side hustle if doing it means you'll never see your kids.

Choose methods for budgeting, spending, and making money that you enjoy. That's why I practice the Simple Spending System: It made me anxious trying to predict what and where I was going to spend every month. I hated it. Creating a plan that allows me to cover the important stuff first and have the freedom to spend the rest as I want brings me joy.

And when all else fails, gratitude is a powerful intrinsic motivator. Feeling grateful changes how you feel about life and increases the joy you feel when you live it. Being intentional to express gratitude daily will make even the dullest tasks feel like a privilege to be able to do.

How to Get and Stay Motivated

Motivation doesn't magically come when you need it. You have to be proactive about setting up external rewards and cultivating internal ones. Here's how:

Schedule it.

You can make the reservation for that reward dinner in advance or write down on the calendar the exact time you're making your extra debt payment.

Make it a game.

Challenge yourself to stop spending for a week or to make $1000 in your side hustle this month. Gamifying difficult changes can take the sting off and increase motivation.

Read a book or take a course.

Knowledge isn't motivating but the process of learning new things can motivate you to stick to whatever you're doing. And bonus, personal finance books are cheap. Heck, they're free if you have a library card!

Help others.

Starting my blog to help others motivated me to keep going more than anything. If writing isn't your thing, record podcasts or YouTube videos. Helping others learn the lessons you've already implemented is a powerful motivator.

Take care of yourself.

Exercise consistently, eliminate stress, eat your greens, and get as much sleep as you can. Keeping your body and mind at peak performance will help you think clearer and make better decisions.

How to Persevere When You're Not Motivated

Sometimes the perfect storm arises and you'd rather not get out of bed, much less plan meals or cook the actual meals. On those days you need to be able to push through without motivation.

Tackle the worst first. This concept comes from Brian Tracy's book, Eat That Frog! By tackling your least favorite task first, you can stop procrastinating and get more done even when you don't feel like doing anything.

Start small. Maybe you're in Target and you have several items in your cart that you did not go in there for. Instead of putting them all back, put one thing back. You don't have to be perfect when you're in a rut, but make a small effort to stay on track.

Fake it 'til you make it. Everyone who's ever done anything big has had to pretend they're doing well when they're not. There will be times you'll have to drag yourself out of the house to deliver pizzas or begrudgingly eat the food in your fridge. But rest assured, if you can push through these moments and keep following through, you will find your motivation again.

Motivation is integral in sustaining your debt-free journey but don't expect to be perfect. Your struggles and motivations will evolve as you progress. Always be willing to change things up as you grow.

Today's Action Steps:
- Determine extrinsic motivators for little and big accomplishments.
- Write down the things that you're internally motivated by.

DAY 11

BUILD BETTER HABITS

When your brain gets tired, it goes on autopilot and you find yourself doing the things that are easy to do instead of the things you want to do.

I always have good intentions of getting work done after my baby goes to bed. But when eight o'clock rolls around, I always find myself on the couch with a glass of wine, nowhere near my computer.

My "wine on the couch" habit isn't my best one, but I have plenty of other good habits built up to compensate. That's because I've found that forming healthy habits makes life so much easier in the long run.

95

Especially if you don't want to have to think about paying off debt 24/7.

A habit is defined as a behavior that has become nearly or completely involuntary. You probably don't even realize most of your habits. I had a habit of stopping at Chipotle after staying out late or having a stressful day at work. When I started working extra hours, my paycheck got bigger but I noticed my spending at Chipotle increased with it. When my motivation and energy were gone, my habit took over.

What makes sticking to a budget difficult aren't the limits you set, but rather the day-to-day spending habits that take over when you're tired. Those habits derail your carefully calculated plans.

We need habits because our brain can only work at a certain capacity every day. There are going to be times you're beat and all you can do is coast through. With healthy habits in place, you can still make good decisions on those days like making coffee at home or bringing leftovers for lunch.

And it's important to note that paying off debt is only a temporary goal (regardless of how long you think it'll take you.) Good money habits will carry you beyond debt freedom and into serious wealth-building. Understanding healthy habits will also help you reach your fitness, family, and career goals.

Forming Healthy Habits

I used to think we needed to focus on breaking bad money habits before building good ones. After reading a lot about habits, I now know the best way to start is with the positive.

Habits are formed by voluntary routines that over time become automatic. That means any voluntary routine practiced over and over can become a habit. You need to have good routines and practices in place before you eliminate the bad ones.

Building good habits can feel inconvenient, but it shouldn't feel hard. Here's how to do it in a way that's manageable.

1. Start simple.

Pick one habit at a time to build. Here's why: In habit psychology there's a concept called ego depletion. It's the idea that you have a finite amount of mental energy to execute self-control and willpower. Once your mental energy is low, your brain can't execute self-control anymore. That state of low mental energy is ego depletion.

Starting simple will limit your ego depletion and allow you to have more willpower and self-control to build the habit you've chosen. I recommend starting with one habit, but if you're really excited you can start with two. Examples could be:

- Making daily debt payments
- Tracking your spending every night
- Gradually increasing your savings or debt payments
- Shopping at more affordable stores
- Checking daily or weekly with your accountability partner

- Saying "no" to yourself (and your kids)
- Giving or donating regularly
- Waking up an hour early
- Getting to work 15 minutes early

Focus your motivation on one or two habits for as long as it takes for them to become automatic. Then you can add more.

2. Make it a routine.

Routines are what make a new habit habitual. For most of these, you can't get away with practicing them once or twice a week. For fast results, you have to do it daily.

To make it easier, attach the habit you're trying to create to a habit that's already established. You're already going to wake up in the morning, wake up early to work on your side hustle. Or while you're brushing your teeth at night with one hand, log your transactions for the day in the other.

This method is called habit stacking, and it's a simple way to build upon healthy habits or replace bad ones, which we'll talk about soon.

3. Make it attractive.

One way to avoid giving into temptation is make whatever you know you should be doing tempting as well. Find a way to enjoy the thing that's good for you and you'll find it's much easier to follow through.

To make a new habit more attractive, James Clear's book Atomic Habits recommends bundling it with something you enjoy doing. Like if you love podcasts, make a rule you can only listen to podcasts while you're doing your side hustle or decluttering your house. It's like a reward system for completing your habit.

This can be done in tandem with habit stacking. If you look forward to scrolling Instagram in the evening, make a rule that you can't scroll until your transactions for the day are logged. So every night you brush your teeth, log your daily spending, and then you can veg out on Instagram.

4. Commit to at least 30 days.

The amount of time it takes to form a new habit varies based on the habit. Easier habits, like changing where you buy groceries, take less time to form. Cooking at home is much harder and takes longer to become habit.

By committing to at least 30 days you may not solidify your new habit, but you will set yourself on the path to doing so. Make committing as easy as possible by putting the task on your schedule. Make it a priority.

Studies show people who make a plan and schedule things in advance follow through more often than those who don't. Automate as much as you can, schedule grocery pick-ups to stay out of the store, and write things down in your calendar.

5. Surround yourself with positive reinforcement.

There's power in numbers. Spend time with people who share your values and want you to succeed. You're more likely to become frugal in an environment of people who are, or are trying to become, frugal.

Don't waste your energy on people who will help you rationalize skipping a day or aren't supportive. If those people are family or coworkers and you know they have to be in your life, use the 30-day commitment as an excuse to see them less. You don't have to tell them what you're doing, just that your commitments have you tied up until a certain date.

Lastly, give yourself grace. You won't be perfect, you will mess up, and that's OK. One step backward after two steps forward is still progress. We're not trying to break any records for fastest human transformation, so go at your pace and don't be bummed about your mistakes for too long.

Today's Action Step:

- Determine the one or two habits you want to start building and schedule them into your day. You can do this on the Day 11 worksheet in your free workbook. Find it at modernfrugality.com/debtfreeworkbook.

DAY 12

BREAK BAD HABITS

I was never a big fast-food fan, but when I had my baby in the blistering heat of summer in Florida, my new daily outing became sitting in drive thrus. He cried for the first two months of his life and only stopped if he was in the car seat. It was too hot to take a walk and making food was difficult with a screaming baby, so there I sat, eating my bacon burger in silence.

Then the crying stopped, mostly, and I still found myself in those drive thrus because by that point it had become part of my day.

I'm happy to say I'm eating far fewer fast food hamburgers nowadays but it shows that no matter how well you know the science behind good habits, you're not immune from bad ones.

You'll continue to find new ones creep up and old ones make a comeback. By being able to look at bad habits objectively and have routines in place for eliminating them, you can get back on track faster. Here's how:

1. Identify the habit and underlying cause.

What financial habits are you dealing with? And why did you adopt them in the first place? The first step in breaking a bad habit is to write it down and dig deep in search of why you do it. Some examples are:

- Impulse buying
- Ignoring bills and debt
- Maxing out credit cards
- Spending your whole paycheck
- "Keeping up with the Joneses"
- Shopping because you're mad/sad/anxious/ happy/etc.

105

Before paying off my debt I had a problem spending every penny of my paycheck. For some reason I could not let money sit in my bank account. If it was there, I had to spend it. That went for cash in my wallet too. For the longest time I couldn't understand why I did this. When I sat down to focus on it, it actually didn't take me long to follow the trail back and figure out why.

When I was growing up, we never took family vacations, fixed up our house, or did anything that required saving. Instead, my mom and I went shopping and ate out a lot. Those activities didn't require saving.

In adulthood I had a scarcity mindset. No matter what my income, I never thought I'd have enough money to save for big things or to pay off my debt — even when I got a raise and a second job — so I just spent my whole paycheck on meaningless stuff.

Chances are, a few of your money habits stem from your childhood as well. And maybe you can't nail down just one reason for your habit; it's okay to have a few. The important exercise here is to start to identify those underlying causes so you can move on to step two.

2. Deal with the underlying cause/problem.

Once you figure out that you go to Starbucks three times a week as an excuse to get out of the office, you realize you don't have a Starbucks problem, you actually have a problem with being stuck in your office all day.

You need to figure out why you need to get out of the office every afternoon. Is it because you have an overbearing boss? Or do you enjoy the fresh air after completing your morning tasks?

For my spending habit, I had to confront my scarcity mindset. It was a long, sucky process. And truthfully, I am still working on it. But I've taken the unhealthy version of it and replaced it with something better.

3. Replace the unhealthy habit.

When I worked in health care, I saw a lot of patients who wanted to quit smoking. I would tell them the story of my dad, who quit smoking cold-turkey by replacing cigarettes with popsicles. As a kid I remember thinking "Is he addicted to popsicles now?"

Addiction was only a fraction of the problem, the habit was the real monster he needed to beat. So he found an activity that was similar, but healthier, and replaced it.

For my spending problem, I replaced spending my whole paycheck on stuff to spending it all on debt. I found that it gave me the same (weird) satisfaction of seeing my bank account empty, but without all the guilt.

Your replacement might be finding another way to cope with your emotions besides shopping, or using your debit card instead of your credit card. Figure out a way that you can replace your unhealthy action with a healthy one. It doesn't have to be the healthiest new habit, just something healthier than the old one.

4. Remove triggers.

I love the phrase "work smarter, not harder." Don't make yourself do hard things just to say you persevered.

Remove the triggers that will lead you to fall back onto your bad habits. If you leave the office in the afternoon and know you'll go to Starbucks if you pass by one, walk another way. If you're going to spend all the money in your bank account on clothes, take the money out of your bank account before you have the chance to go shopping.

Don't feel like because you're on this road to self-improvement that you have to be instantly strong and controlled. You're not. Set your life up to avoid temptation and you have a far better chance at success than if you keep everything the same.

5. Be patient.

Just because you have the knowledge doesn't mean you have the willpower to execute it perfectly. Just like building good habits, breaking bad habits takes time. Allow for slips, confide in your accountability partner, and be kind to yourself.

It's never too late to break a habit. Habits are ever-changing, and only you can decide whether they change for the better.

The Importance of Resilience in Forming Habits

Ever wonder how some people make paying off debt look so easy even when everything's working against them, while others just can't seem to get it together? There may be more to it than what you see on the surface.

Researchers have observed that if you followed two children with similar ages and early childhood experience, one could go on to be successful while the other struggled consistently. They found it wasn't the experience or their upbringing that determined their future actions. It was each child's internal resilience.

Psychological resilience is the ability to get knocked down by life and bounce back as strong as (or stronger than) before. In the end, the researchers determined children who had naturally independent personalities developed resilience instinctually while others didn't.

Fortunately, researchers found that even if you didn't naturally develop resilience as a child, it's never too late to build it. By reframing your mindset to believe that you, not your circumstances, affect your achievement, you can become resilient.

By viewing adverse events as opportunities to learn and grow as opposed to traumatic setbacks that are being done to you, you'll form your own resiliency and feel more in control of your life.

If you feel like you keep falling back into old habits again and again, and you give up or have a hard time coping when things set you back, you may need to work on your resiliency.

Every time you feel like something bad is happening to you, step back and identify how you came to be in your current situation and how you can get out of it. Don't make excuses, make progress. Eventually resiliency will be another good habit in your repertoire.

Today's Action Step:
- Identify one bad habit you want to break and take steps to replace it.

DAY 13

CONTROL THE BIG FOUR

When I decided to start paying off my debt, I thought I could earn my way out. I took on several side jobs and worked 12 hours a day for a few months. Unfortunately, my body didn't share the same vigor, and two months into this routine I got shingles—a fiery, stabbing, blister-filled rash all over the left side of my ribs.

Realizing my body literally wouldn't allow me to outearn my spending was a turning point. I knew I needed to swallow my pride and start saying "no" to all the unnecessary things I was spending money on.

But to my surprise, avoiding Starbucks and the Target dollar section wasn't enough to make a dent in my budget. It actually caused more stress that I felt needed to be resolved with more lattes.

I came to the realization that it's not the $3 and $4 decisions that move the needle; it's the $300 and $400 ones.

The choices you make on your largest expenses are the most impactful to your debt-free journey. They will determine the speed at which you finish paying your debt. Working 10 side hustles is nice for a few weeks, but lowering the cost of where you live, how you get to work, or the phone service you use has a huge impact on your bank account while changing little in your day-to-day routine.

The four biggest slices of your expense pie are housing, recurring bills, transportation, and food. One or two changes in each of these categories can save you hundreds of dollars per month. If you start with one change now and make one more every month, in six months you could cut your monthly expenses by $1,000.

Before you say things like "I can't change where I live" or "I need this car," be open to having your mind changed. You may not be able to give up your car or move into a studio apartment, but I guarantee there's at least one thing you can do to lower your costs in each of these categories.

Housing

Housing should be the first place you look to spend less. It's no doubt the hardest place to cut but even the slightest change can make a big impact.

In 2019, the average cost to rent a two-bedroom apartment in the U.S. was $1,190 per month. What you really pay varies state-to-state: the same apartment might cost $437 in Alabama and $4,683 in California.

If you could find rent that's $100 cheaper per month or find a way to cover $100 of your mortgage, you could save $1,200 in a year. Bump that number up to $200 per month and that's an extra $2,400 to put toward your debt. You can't give up enough lattes to equal that.

For Renters

Consider moving to a less expensive neighborhood as long as you don't make up the costs in transportation. If you could move 10 minutes further outside the city but closer to the interstate you can save money on rent without changing your commute time by much.

Also, try downsizing for a few years. You may think you need a guest room, but really, how often do you have guests? Could you go from 1200 square feet to 900? Or 750? You can live in a small space for a short amount of time. It's not ideal, but it's also not forever.

For those who do have a lot of guests or need an office to justify that guest room, see if your lease allows you to rent out the room or your entire apartment on Airbnb. We rent our spare room out for $35 to $40 per night and can make well over $500 in a slow month. And if you go out of town frequently, you could rent the whole apartment for a higher rate.

You could also get a roommate. This is usually the first option people think about and subsequently where they stop. I put it last because I want you to see there are other ways to cut your housing costs if you don't want a roommate. But if none of those options suit you, you may need to think about getting one.

For Homeowners

Depending on the equity you have, it may make sense to refinance your home. It's a small investment up front, but you can lower your monthly payment and typically break even in about three years. If refinancing doesn't save you money right now, rent out space in your home or on your property.

Check your local laws to see if you can rent out a room or your whole house on Airbnb. It only takes a few days a month to supplement your payment by hundreds of dollars.

If Airbnb is out of the question, there are websites that allow you to post your pool for parties, driveway for parking, garage for storage, or a spare bedroom as studio space. There are dozens of ways you turn underutilized space into profit. You're not looking to build a business, just to make a couple hundred dollars per month to offset your housing costs.

For Aspiring Homeowners

When you look at houses, don't just look at single-family homes and condos. Consider a multi-unit property. When you purchase a duplex, triplex, or four-unit building, and live in one unit while renting out the rest, the renters will essentially end up paying for your mortgage.

It's called house hacking, and it's the closest thing to living mortgage-free that you can get outside of living with your parents.

Transportation

Real estate investors have a saying: "Your money is made on the purchase." That means no matter how great the house is, you'll never make your money back if you don't get a great deal on the purchase of a house.

The same is true when saving money on transportation. Your money is saved when you buy (or don't buy) a car. Buying cheaper gas, changing your own oil, and parking further away are trivial expenses when you consider how much you save by purchasing the right car.

Saving Money on a Car

As of 2019, the average car payment is $554 for a new vehicle and $391 for a used vehicle. That doesn't include any other costs associated with owning a car.

If you're a two-car family, experiment with using only one for a month to see if you can sell the other. Move your schedule around, find carpool opportunities, and try some alternative transportation. Many households overestimate their need for two cars and could live with just one without a ton of effort. As a perk, you'll spend less on gas during the experiment.

For those who need two cars, drive low-cost, reliable used cars. For example, if you purchase a reliable car for $5,000 and sell it later for $2,500, your total investment should be around $3,000, since reliable cars at that price usually don't need more than regular maintenance and replacements. If you drive that car for three years, or any longer than 30 months, you're paying less than $100 per month for a car. That's a savings of at least $300 per month compared to buying a new car.

What are these reliable used cars? Toyotas and Hondas top the list, but you can see a few other models from various brands on Kelley Blue Book.

You're not likely to get a $5,000 car from a dealership, so your best bet is to go to a private seller. Facebook Marketplace and listing sites like CarGurus are best. If you choose to go to a dealer, don't bother haggling in person. You can negotiate faster and more easily from the comfort of your home.

Choose the car you want and email several dealers about the closest one they have. Ask for their best offer, what extras they can include, and best financing rates if you're going that route. You can usually get at least $500 off the list price from everyone and make the dealers compete with each other for your business before you ever step foot on a lot.

For Alternative Commuters

Want to save even more? Skip the car.

In America's most expensive city to take public transit, Los Angeles, you'll pay $122 for an unlimited monthly pass. Add a few Uber rides per month to that cost and you're still well under the average used car payment.

The average cost of a monthly transit pass in the U.S. is closer to $67 per month. Meaning you could spend $300 per month on ridesharing and still spend less than the average used car payment, and you never have to worry about remembering to pay your auto insurance.

Try a combination of alternative transportation methods, just for a month. Bike more, ride the bus, and get on a first name basis with your rideshare drivers to see how much you could save without a car.

Bills

Unplugging your appliances every night won't save you significant money on your energy bill. It'll just annoy you in the morning when you have to reset all the digital clocks. What will save you money is choosing the right plans and staying on top of them.

Shop around for deals on all your services. Call providers once a year to see who can give you the best rate. It'll take some time on the phone, but companies will compete to get and keep your business, and that results in lower rates.

You can also raise the deductibles on your insurance plans. Health insurance is another large monthly expense, and while you often can't change your insurance provider, you can adjust your plan during open enrollment. If you're healthy with no major procedures planned, choose a high deductible health plan with a health savings account (HSA) or flexible spending account (FSA). The monthly premium will be lower and the contributions you make to your HSA and FSA are pre-tax, meaning you can keep about 25 cents more per dollar.

Food

Learning the skills of meal planning, meal prepping, and repurposing leftovers will save you lots of money. I talk all about this in my book, Meal Planning on a Budget.

But even with those skills, the two biggest things that keep people from eating at home are time and skill. And I'd say that it's lack of skill that contributes to the amount of time it takes to cook.

The best thing you can do for your future grocery bills is to learn how to cook and learn to love it. You can take a class, but everything you need to learn basic cooking skills is available for free on the internet, specifically YouTube.

You can search for instructions on anything related to cooking and find a variety of YouTubers with professional tutorials that will help you and inspire you to cook more. Everyone has a different food personality. Learn yours by watching different chefs cook different dishes and you'll gain a passion for cooking at home that won't just save you money, but will also enrich your relationships with family, friends, and your health.

I've listed some of my favorite YouTube cooks on my website. You can find it in the resource page for this book. Watch them whenever you have a little extra time and become the home chef you were meant to be!

Today's Action Steps:

- Using your Financial Inventory, choose one of your biggest areas of spending to start cutting down.

- Try one of the suggestions from this chapter for cutting your spending in that category.

DAY 14

CREATE SHORT-TERM INCOME

Some people might disagree, but fundamentally, cutting your spending is easier than increasing your income. But while you should start by spending less money, you shouldn't stop there.

Bringing in income above and beyond your salary will skyrocket the rate at which you can pay off your debt. Saving money is typically finite; you save $100 this month and next month you'll be saving the same $100. When you're making money, you can make $100 this month and go up every month from there.

But you can also go down, too. So it's important to view the income differently for different purposes.

126

Why Short-Term Income Is Important

Making money quickly requires a different strategy than long-term wealth building does.

Because your immediate goal is to pay off debt, we'll start with that type of income. I refer to it as short-term income.

Short-term income is money that can be made fast and often but can't be relied upon forever.

Driving for a rideshare company is the perfect example of short-term income. You can sign up and start driving quickly and in some markets get paid the same day you drive. You can work as often as you want, whenever you want and make a decent wage doing it.

The drawback is, in order to make decent money you'll have to work at inconvenient hours, like at 2 a.m. when the bars are closing. There's no room for growth if you're a good driver, and Uber could change its payout and fee structure whenever it wants without consulting you.

Long-term types of income can certainly make you enough to become debt free. But they take time and monetary investment to build—things you don't necessarily have while paying off debt quickly.

Doing one-off jobs for people isn't consistent and can't be done often. Taking surveys or participating in rewards apps can be done fast and often, but doesn't produce anywhere near the payoff required to make them worth the time you put in.

When considering whether you should take a side job or start a side hustle run it through this filter:

- Can I start fast?
- Can I do it often?
- Can I make at least $12- $15 per hour doing it?

Some good examples of short-term income sources are rideshare driving, dog walking, food delivery, teaching English, babysitting, and cleaning houses. An easy way to see if something you want to do can be short-term income is to search the web for a company that offers those services. For all the jobs I mentioned above, there are websites you can sign up for and offer those services through.

Going It Alone

When you're starting out paying off your debt, I strongly recommend working with an established company so you can get your feet wet and quickly feel the satisfaction of seeing those extra dollars come in.

But once you've done it for a while, you don't have to keep paying someone else for the exposure you could be getting on your own. You'll know it's time to go it alone when you've built up enough word of mouth exposure that people start asking you for your services outside of the website or app.

Word of mouth is a powerful marketing tool, and it's free. If you're walking dogs, tell people on social media, share pictures, tell stories, print some free business cards to give to clients. Do a great job with your current customers and they'll tell their friends. It'll take time, but eventually you'll be able to make money fast and frequently on your own.

Today's Action Step:

- Brainstorm side-hustle ideas. You can do this on the Day 14 worksheet in the free workbook that accompanies this book. Find it at modernfrugality.com/debtfreeworkbook.

DAY 15

THINK ABOUT LONG-TERM INCOME

Short-term income is the income that's going to move the needle on your debt repayment. But your financial life doesn't end when you finish paying off your debt.

It takes off.

Paying off your debt changes the way you make, save, and spend money. It sets the foundation for a life where you can pay for vacations in cash, put the 20% down payment on your house, and max out your tax-advantaged retirement accounts. It also sets the foundation to care about what that last one means.

131

Your debt-free journey is like driving an old car. It takes a long time to get from zero to 60, and once it's there you don't want to pump the brakes too hard because cruising at that speed feels good!

So it makes sense that the question I hear most from people who are close to or who have paid off their debt is, "How do I keep this momentum?"

You do it by thinking about your next move now.

Like I mentioned yesterday, saving money is finite, but making money is forever. In addition to the short-term income that's speeding up your debt payoff, start to think about and build your long term income.

The Difference Between Millionaires and The Middle Class

There's a book I love titled The Top 10 Distinctions Between Millionaires and the Middle Class, by Keith Cameron Smith. His book showed me some of the money mindsets my middle class upbringing instilled in me that were holding me back from being successful with money.

The first distinction is that millionaires think long-term while the middle class thinks short-term. Shifting this mindset is the starting point for achieving success.

Planning for the next car you'll drive and the first debt-free vacation you'll save for is great, but millionaires don't think about saving this way. They think, how can I double my income next year? What's my five-year business plan? How much do I want in my tax-advantaged retirement account in 30 years?

I want you to start thinking like this. Because when you work toward bigger goals, you achieve smaller goals simultaneously. And when your mind is on the big picture, small setbacks don't seem as significant. When you focus your momentum on things with lasting value, you won't have to worry about ending up back where you started. So start thinking about the long term while you're paying off your debt.

How to Create Lasting Value

Ever wonder how millionaires get a million dollars? I used to think the secret was high six-figure salaries or rich parents. Or maybe they invented something and had outside investors. With that mindset I assumed I'd never be a millionaire.

Even when I started investing for retirement, I calculated I wouldn't hit $1 million until I turned 65.

To my surprise, I learned that most millionaires don't come from money or do anything radical to accumulate their wealth. I also learned that I don't have to wait until my 60s to get there.

We assume our salary and side hustles are the only way to make money, but millionaires have an average of seven income streams. That doesn't mean they work seven jobs—it means they've diversified their income over several different sources of revenue. If one fails, they have six others to sustain them. They're always thinking about creating value that lasts, never relying on one thing.

That's a mistake we often make. We think the next big thing will be the thing that'll set us up for life. Millionaires know that every business is fleeting, so when one thing is successful it's time to start thinking about the next.

So while you're riding the momentum of paying off your debt, it's time to start thinking about your next thing.

Not only does it prepare you for the day you become debt free; it's giving you another source of intrinsic and extrinsic motivation. Intrinsic in that it gives you the opportunity to explore hobbies, passions, and ideas you like. Extrinsic in that these things are hopefully going to lead to wealth someday.

And there's no better time to start than right now, because you don't have the luxury of investing a lot of money in a venture that won't work. Starting without a significant monetary investment forces you to get creative with how you begin and allows you to more easily abandon ideas that aren't working.

Here's how to start working on your long-term income without a big investment of time or money.

1. Make a list of your hobbies, interests, and passions.
2. Research how other people are monetizing those things.
3. Start doing something small to become more knowledgeable and proficient in your craft.
4. Share your skills and ideas with others to gauge interest.

Here's how it worked for me: One of my passions is writing. While I was paying off debt I wanted to help people and try to monetize my love of writing. So I started my blog which eventually became Modern Frugality.

The blog allowed me to practice my writing but it wasn't making me a lot of money. However, it allowed me to see that people did enjoy my writing style. So I shifted my focus and wrote The No-Spend Challenge Guide, Meal Planning on a Budget, and the book you're reading now. It took me several years from start to publish to make any money, but now my books have produced tens of thousands of dollars of profit with very little ongoing work.

So do your debt-free self a huge service by planning for your future wealth. And know the thing you're working on today probably won't be the thing that launches you to millionaire status. But you'll never get to seven income streams without first working toward one.

Today's Action Steps:

- Write your list of hobbies, passions, and skills.
- Research and brainstorm ways to monetize your favorites.

DAY 16

FORTIFY YOUR RELATIONSHIPS

When I started changing the way I spent money, something that never crossed my mind to think about was how it would affect my relationships. I knew I'd be going out less, buying fewer drinks, and taking fewer trips, but I really only thought about my spending in the context of how it would impact me.

What I quickly realized is that the choices I was making to become debt free also impacted the people on the other side of those relationships: my family, friends, and spouse.

I navigated situations and made mistakes during those years that I wouldn't wish on anyone. I felt isolated, angry, judgmental, and remorseful all because of decisions I made to prioritize paying off debt.

But those years were also transformative for some relationships. I made friends and strengthened relationships with people who shared my values. They've now become some of my closest friends. And I've set healthy boundaries with family members that have saved me endless amounts of stress today.

This debt-free journey can fortify your relationships across the board, but you have to be willing to let go of some. There are also things you can do differently than I did to experience less tension and show more grace.

Your Marriage or Partnership

Your partner, the person you're closest to. The one that knows you best, for better or for worse. This can be the hardest or easiest relationship to deal with, but it always has to be first.

Unlike friends and family who don't have to agree with what you're doing, if your partner isn't yet on board with paying off debt, you'll want to get them there in at least some capacity. If that's your goal, here are some important reminders for talking and doing life with them.

Be honest. Tell them why you're doing this crazy thing. They don't need to hear numbers, they need to hear you. And when you mess up, be honest and show them you're committed by getting right back up and picking up where you left off. Perfection doesn't inspire, perseverance does.

Be kind. Your spouse may have irresponsible spending habits or be unmotivated at their job, but yelling and judgement won't change their behavior. Be kind in your words and actions toward them, even when their financial choices frustrate you. Kindness doesn't mean being a pushover—be firm in moving toward your goals. Instead of taking out your anger on your spouse, you may need to seek counseling to get better at communicating with each other.

Be patient. Mindsets don't change overnight. Be consistent and persistent for as long as it takes. Know that it might take longer than you think it should but continue to lead by example and your partner will come around.

If both you and your partner are committed to paying off debt, you're not off the hook for some tough lessons.

One time I bought a first run distillation of vodka from a new distillery in our city. As a former bartender, I'm a big fan of nice liquors. But I didn't plan on drinking it and it wasn't in our budget, so I hid it from my husband. The problem was, we lived in less than 700 square feet. It took him less than 24 hours to find it.

I don't remember how much the bottle cost, but I vividly remember the look on his face when I told him. He wasn't mad that I'd bought it, but he was confused and hurt that I thought I needed to hide it from him. And from that day I never hid any purchase from him again, no matter how embarrassing.

For a couple who paid off $78,000 of debt, we still argue about money more than anything else in our relationship. That comes with the territory of being open about it. We know ourselves and we're brutally honest about how we want and don't want to spend money.

Don't be afraid to disagree. Instead, use those disagreements to learn each other's strengths and weaknesses to become a stronger team when handling money together.

Friendships

College was the first time I felt like I'd found "my people." They were the kind of friends that understood me without saying anything, made me laugh like crazy, and were there in bad times as much as the good.

After college, we scattered throughout the state, close enough to see each other regularly but far enough that you had to spend the whole day and some money to do it. So when we decided to pay off debt, side jobs filled my weekends and road trips got cut out of the budget.

At that time, none of my friends were paying off debt or living on a tight budget, and for two years I watched my best friends get together frequently without me. I joined in occasionally, but it wasn't the same, and I could feel us slowly growing apart. I even had to unfollow one friend on social media because her pictures made me jealous and miserable.

It also forced me to make new friends that lived closer to me. Ones that I could invite over to drink a $3 bottle of wine on a weeknight or attend a free event on the weekend. These friends didn't expect anything from me because they didn't know any other side of me, and they made those two years bearable.

Whether you're married or single, paying off debt can be painfully isolating. If you want to sustain the several years it's going to take you to become debt free and maintain a financially smart lifestyle beyond it, you need quality friends for the journey.

That means giving up some relationships and finding new ones, at least for now.

Fast forward: My college friends are all still my best friends. And that friend I had to unfollow? Now she's paying off debt and living on a budget, and we have a great relationship. And my new friends are still some of my favorite people.

I wish I'd known then what I know now. That real friendships stand the test of time and the ones that don't aren't worth it. And that I may have missed out on some great friends if I hadn't been looking for relationships that would take me further.

You'll find the same thing. When you change how you make and spend your money, your relationships will change too. Don't be afraid of the change.

Family

When I think about how my immediate family and in-laws affect my finances I immediately think about Christmas.

144

My side of the family is just my mom and me. My husband's parents are divorced and remarried, so he has multiple large families that all live within an hour of us. Christmas is insane.

We will never have enough money to buy presents for everyone who gets us gifts each Christmas, and when we were paying off debt, we had to draw a hard line about for whom we would buy presents.

We were honest with our families and thankfully didn't get too much push back. But not every family is so understanding. Family members have expectations about how holidays, birthdays, and special events should be celebrated. It's your responsibility to gently guide those expectations to reality.

You can do this by setting boundaries with your family. Boundaries are rules, guidelines, or limits you set that give you permission to pull back when things are about to go too far. Loving your family well and prioritizing your needs are not mutually exclusive, and boundaries will help you do both.

We still only buy presents for our immediate relatives. That's our limit and we're honest with our families about it. We also reserve the right to skip a family reunion if we want or not attend one of the numerous family gatherings if we don't want to go. Our boundaries mean seeing our family is never something we do begrudgingly, but always something we want to do and can afford to participate in.

Setting boundaries is easy. Enforcing them usually isn't. When instituting boundaries:

Be firm, but kind. You may deal with family members who try to guilt you into lending money to someone or pitching in on a gift you can't afford. Understand where they're coming from, but continue to stick to your budget.

Keep expectations realistic. If you're someone who has always bought gifts for everyone, it may take you several years to work down to only buying gifts for your immediate family. Don't expect everyone to be OK with your new rule, even people who you thought wouldn't care.

You can choose your friends, but you can't choose your family. Protect these relationships so they can be a source of joy in your life, instead of the stress they cause so many people.

Today's Action Steps:
- Talk with your partner about your debt-free journey.
- Plan on how you'll set boundaries with unsupportive friends and family.
- Identify some frugal friends you'd like to spend more time with.

DAY 17

DECLUTTER YOUR SURROUNDINGS

Decluttering your surroundings might seem trivial, but it plays an important role in your path to debt freedom.

Clutter is distracting. Things upon things force your brain to multitask and make focusing virtually impossible. And when you're trying to reach a goal as multifaceted as paying off debt, you need to make focusing as easy as possible.

Having less stuff also cuts down on your desire to purchase more. It seems counterintuitive, but clutter actually tells your brain you always need "one more thing" to pull the room together. On the other hand, a minimalist lifestyle trains you to think, "what can I take away so I'm only left with things I absolutely love?"

You'll learn more and more about yourself as you get rid of the unused stuff you thought you needed and start displaying the things that make life easier.

The process will take a while and won't always be fun, but add it to your calendar and make it a priority. You'll probably find yourself wanting to keep more at first, but the further you are in this journey the more freedom you'll feel to let go of at least some of your material items.

Here's a guide to minimizing your belongings while you minimize your debt. The worst mistake you can make is decluttering an entire room, but then having boxes of things to sell next to bags of things to donate, all sitting around for weeks. Start with a small area and finish all the steps before going on to the next.

1. Clear the Clutter

Your house doesn't have to look like an episode of Hoarders to be full of clutter. It's in your closets and drawers, it's on your shelves and counters. Clutter is any extra stuff that doesn't serve the area it's in.

When you're decluttering an area, take away everything that doesn't belong there. You can use the KonMari method and choose only to keep what sparks joy. Or if you're more practical, you can just get rid of things you haven't used recently. Choose whatever decluttering method works for you.

2. Clean What's Left

The next step, and understandably the easiest to skip, is clean what you keep. You're there anyway! There will never be an easier time to get a rag and wipe the dust off your books or the grease out of your cupboards.

And let's face it, you're going out less, which means you're spending more time at home. That shouldn't be a source of suffering. Create clean spaces in your home that you enjoy being in, and it'll make staying in easier to do.

Also good to note: The less you have, the less you have to clean in the future, and the easier it is to clean it. Cleaning it now will give you a realistic expectation of how much time it'll take to clean your whole decluttered house later.

3. Organize

Once everything's clean, organize it. Psychologists who have studied occupational health have found that the more control you feel like you have in your work, the more job satisfaction and less stress you're likely to experience.

Organization gives you a sense of control over your household. When you put things in places that make sense and you know where they are, you worry less about whether you have something, and buy fewer duplicates. As an added bonus, you'll like the way things look together.

4. Sell

Once you've decided what you don't need, sell as much of it as you can and put the money toward your debt. As of this writing, Facebook Marketplace is easiest place to sell items locally. If the items you have are more niche, eBay is a great place to find buyers looking for unique things.

You can easily make hundreds of dollars to put toward your debt by decluttering your home, and in the process you'll create a space you'll want to spend time in and invite people into.

Today's Action Step:

- Start with one drawer. Clear it, clean it, and organize it.

DAY 18

SIMPLIFY YOUR ONLINE PRESENCE

Technology is a blessing and a curse. We're more connected than ever, and daily life is easier thanks to technology. But it's the same technology that divides, isolates, and stresses us, often causing us to spend money that we otherwise wouldn't.

In his book Digital Minimalism, Cal Newport outlines a philosophy for using technology as much as we need but not as much as we want. Digital minimalism isn't about giving up your smartphone or deleting Facebook. It's about focusing and optimizing your online time to serve you best.

Simplifying your online presence can help you regain control over your time with family and friends instead of checking your likes and comments. It allows you to fully optimize a few tools instead of having dozens you barely open. And you can kiss your FOMO goodbye.

On a practical level, it also minimizes personalized advertising, prevents you from seeing the "Joneses" you might want to keep up with, and cuts down on time you might fill with "browsing" online shopping sites.

Commit to 30 days of cutting out all optional technologies in your life. During the break, you'll learn what makes your life easier and what's just taking up space. Here's how you can go about simplifying your online presence to help you pay off your debt.

Social Media

As much as I wish I could give up social media, I actually need it for my business. But using it effectively can quickly transition to me scrolling mindlessly through baby pictures and memes and ending an hour later with dishes and laundry still piled high.

So instead of turning to social media as a time filler, use it intentionally. Schedule times where you'll check your accounts, respond to people, and wish happy birthdays. And during all other times of day, don't open the apps.

The iPhone has a feature called Screen Time that allows you to set a time limit for how long social media or other types of apps can be open each day. Once you hit your limit it blocks you from opening the app. Another trick to being on social media less is to post less. Go dark for a week and see how much less time you spend not checking likes and comments.

When you're on social media, there will always be people posting about their new car or vacation. Don't be afraid of hitting the unfollow button if these people make you feel bad. You can always follow them again once you're debt free.

Subscriptions

Email subscriptions can be great for receiving coupons or hearing about sales at places you regularly shop. But they can also tempt you to spend when you shouldn't. I'm a proponent for subscribing to 10-20 businesses that I shop at often, but instead of seeing those emails in my inbox every day, I roll them into one.

I use the free tool Unroll.me to roll all my subscription emails into one daily email. That way I can choose whether I want to see the sales and coupons or not. If I know I need to make a purchase somewhere I can either open my Roll Up and look for the email or search my email inbox for the latest emails from that store inside the Roll Up.

Banking

When you think about digital decluttering, online banking doesn't usually come to mind. But chances are, you have a lot of accounts at different banks and loan servicers. Now is a great time to bring them all together in one app so you can see everything in one place and spend less time logging into different websites.

There are several that do this. I like the app Personal Capital to see all my accounts in one place. From checking and savings to investments and my mortgage, it even uploads my house's current estimated value from Zillow to give me a full picture of my net worth. It's free to use and frequently offers incentives for signing up.

Today's Action Steps:
- Schedule your digital break.
- Unfollow friends who are holding you back.
- Sign up for Personal Capital or a similar all-in-one banking tool.

DAY 19

PROTECT YOUR SCHEDULE

Paying off debt is naturally a busy season. I know I tried to pack in as many things as possible into my schedule to make money and maintain my social life. You may not realize the value in simplifying your schedule yet, but in order to keep your lifestyle sustainable and avoid burnout you need to prioritize it.

That's why it's important to focus on designing a schedule that can sustain fullness while not leaving you to have a mental breakdown in seven months. Because stress not only makes it easier to quit; it also causes you to spend more.

If you've found yourself saying things like:

"I don't have time for a side hustle."

"I'm too busy to cook."

"I'm so tired, I don't know how much longer I can do this."

Then it's time to start pruning your schedule. If there's no time for a side hustle, you'll hold yourself back from your full potential. If there's no time to learn to cook or practice cooking, you'll continue eating out.

Also, the stress an overly packed schedule causes can inhibit decision making, and lets our brain to revert back to the comfortable habits of buying a latte on your break or a new jacket on Amazon.

You can fit anything you want into your schedule...but you can't fit everything. Here's how to grade, prioritize, and refine your schedule so you can maintain it through this busy time in your life.

Bandwidth Blocking

You may have heard of the time blocking method of scheduling where you schedule every detail of your day, down to your meals, so you can utilize every minute.

What we forget when we make our schedule is the mental bandwidth needed for each task. It's easy to schedule your side gig to start immediately after your day job but if you have a big meeting one day and try to transition straight to driving Uber, you're going to be exhausted, more prone to making bad and potentially dangerous decisions.

Instead of looking at a schedule as blocks of time to fill, behavioral scientist Sendhil Mullainathan suggests we look at our schedule like artwork on a wall. Start with the largest pieces, the tasks that require the majority of your mental or physical energy for the day, and then arrange smaller, easier tasks around them. Then fill the rest of the spaces with moderately taxing responsibilities.

That might look giving yourself 20 minutes to eat a sandwich after work so you can recharge before your next job. Or getting your errands out of the way in the morning so you can fully focus on a big project the rest of the day.

I'm a nerd and like to color-code my tasks by the level of energy they demand. The things that require that I be fully energized, like my work, are green, moderate tasks like responding to emails are blue, and easy tasks that I enjoy or can do on autopilot like grocery shopping are purple or yellow. If you've been feeling tired or run down practice bandwidth blocking for several weeks to see if it eliminates some of that exhaustion.

Eliminate the Stress

When you're making a schedule that prioritizes your energy over your time, you might find that your schedule doesn't tetris itself together like it once did. Don't force it. It's very likely you're going to need to quit some activities altogether or for a season to prioritize the tasks that move you closer to debt freedom.

161

Not sure which tasks to eliminate? Start by grading them like this:

A: Helps you pay off debt, and you need it.

B: Helps you pay off debt, and you like it.

C: Doesn't help you pay off debt, but energizes you.

D: Doesn't help you pay off debt, but doesn't hurt either.

F: Doesn't help you pay off debt, and you don't enjoy it.

As and Bs are no-brainers: They're the things that are keeping you alive and getting you closer to debt freedom at the highest rate, like your job, making extra money, eating, and sleeping. These are the staples of your schedule, and they're not going anywhere.

Fs are also no-brainers. They're the things that cost you time or money, don't move you closer to debt freedom, and don't provide you with enough enjoyment to be worth doing. Or worse, they cause you stress that affects other activities in your week.

There are usually activities that you feel obligated to do. Invitations to certain bridal showers or bachelorette parties, volunteering, family activities, or traditions to which you no longer feel a connection. It requires some boldness, but they're the first things to nix from your schedule.

Cs and Ds require some analysis. Cs don't directly correspond to bigger debt payments or lower expenses, but they keep you going. Think self-care, free activities with friends, date nights. Schedule your C activities around your As and Bs, making sure there are enough of them to keep you going but not so many that they compromise more important tasks.

Ds are neutral but walk a fine line between Cs and Fs. You feel good about them, but your participation is still a little obligatory and they're not energizing you or serving your goals. It's difficult, but you have to cut these out if there's no time left after scheduling your A, B, and C tasks.

You might just need to take a break from them and then you can come back in a less busy season. But if these tasks conflict with anything more important, your sanity depends on cutting them out, no matter how small or insignificant you think they might be.

Grading tasks like this will make sure priorities get the most important parts of your day and you eliminate the stressful, time-sucking tasks that make your schedule unsustainable.

Today's Action Steps:

- List your weekly tasks in order of bandwidth and schedule them accordingly.
- Grade the things on your schedule and start to eliminate the Ds and Fs.

DAY 20

PRACTICE SELF-CARE

Now that you have a schedule that prioritizes self-care, it's time for you to start prioritizing it too. By now you should know that when you're depleted your brain doesn't have the energy it needs to make good decisions.

When you're stressed you're going to fall back on familiar habits and those are probably going to be the poor spending habits you've been trying so hard to break. That's why practicing self-care regularly is important to sustaining your debt payoff journey.

First, we should define what self-care is. Self-care is any activity that you do recharge your mental, emotional,

165

and physical health. It's simple and undemanding. My favorite self-care activity is getting eight straight hours of sleep. Thanks to my six-month-old, I haven't experienced it lately but I remember how restorative it felt. But it's important to note that self-care isn't the same for everyone. Lots of people do yoga for self-care. I personally don't get any enjoyment from doing yoga, so that's not self-care for me.

Self-care isn't selfish. I enjoy working out several times per week and I leave my son with my husband when I do. When I feel the guilt or selfishness creep up from time to time, I have to remind myself that working out is my self-care and it's essential to being the best person I can be.

Finding Your Self-Care

Determining your self-care routine means discovering who you are and how far your body can go. As you're on this path you'll learn what self-care methods work for you, how much you need, and how often you need them in order to sustain your debt-free journey and other difficult journeys throughout the rest of your life.

While everyone's self-care is different, there are some basics that are restorative for everyone.

- A healthy diet
- 7-8 hours of sleep
- Exercise: Yoga, CrossFit, running, etc.
- Preventative health care: Annual checkups to put your mind at ease
- Relaxation: Meditation and other restorative exercises
- Relationships: Time with family, friends, and your partner
- Enjoyable activities: Reading, walking in the park, laughing, etc.

Paying off debt doesn't mean you sit around the house, bored out of your mind. Get creative in finding activities that restore you. Facebook is a great way to find free events in your area. So is signing up for your city's events newsletter and checking the newspaper.

As essential as adding self-care to your schedule is, saying "no" is just as important. Create a "no" list with things you don't like to do. That could be those D and F tasks you graded earlier or, if you're like me, yoga.

And be intentional. Self-care is an active choice and you should treat it as such. That might mean literally giving yourself a bedtime so you can get eight hours of sleep. Don't pretend self-care will spontaneously happen. Make it happen.

Reward Yourself

I want to circle back around to when we talked about extrinsic motivation earlier. Rewarding yourself along this journey can be a powerful method of self-care!

Start a tradition of rewarding yourself with a certain reward for every milestone. The milestone and reward for it should be consistent and shouldn't derail your goal. Think about rewards like borrowing a new book from the library for every $1,000 you pay off, or marathoning a season of your favorite show every $5,000.

Brainstorm a tradition you can start to look forward to that increases your motivation and re energizes you for the road ahead.

Today's Action Steps:

- Add a self-care session to your schedule.
- Start a tradition for rewarding milestones.

DAY 21

BE FLEXIBLE

People tend to be overly optimistic about what they can accomplish and how fast they can accomplish it. We underestimate how long a task is going to take even when we have knowledge that similar past events took longer than planned—just ask any general contractor.

I planned on finishing this book a month ago, but I'm just now writing the last chapter.

Things rarely go as planned. That's why expecting obstacles and being flexible when they come is the last, and arguably, the most important part of this 21-day challenge.

When you expect obstacles you can create a plan for them, execute it when they arise, and pivot effectively when necessary. You also avoid a lot of the disappointment that comes with these hurdles.

Without this expectation we risk assuming our way is the only right way to pay off debt, and when things don't go our way we give up and assume it's not possible. Being flexible gives you permission to learn from your mistakes, change when something's not working, and grow from adversity.

It doesn't make the actual task any easier, but it does make it easier to cope when things feel like they aren't going well.

When Life Doesn't Cooperate

Murphy's law states that anything that can go wrong will go wrong. I don't believe life is always that dire, but you should go into your debt-free journey knowing that things outside of your control will go wrong.

The best way to get ahead of these inconveniences is to assess what could go wrong from the beginning. Make a list of things you can anticipate going wrong throughout the next three to five years and write down how you'll deal with it. You're only estimating throughout the time you're paying off your debt—not your whole lifetime—so the list will probably be shorter than you think.

Your emergency fund plays a big role in protecting you when life doesn't cooperate. But your actions in response to these situations are important to plan too.

An appliance will probably need replacing, so plan now how and where you could find a replacement. One of your kids will probably need to go to the hospital, so decide who can watch the other kids while you're there and save a vacation day for it. And your car will probably need a costly repair, so figure out how you'd get to work without it.

If you plan ahead, you'll be able to pivot quickly without stressing yourself out.

And if you are stressed and tired, take a step back. The way you're feeling now is not the way you'll feel for the rest of your journey. We often overestimate how painful a slip-up or hard thing will feel compared to how bad it ends up being, but you won't realize that unless you keep going and find out for yourself.

When You Have an "Off" Moment

There are no "bad" days on the road to debt freedom, only "off" moments. If you think of your setbacks in terms of individual events instead of entire days or weeks, you'll bounce back from them quicker.

When you have an "off" moment, don't let it consume you or be the reason you give up even for a short time. These moments are expected and actually a necessary part of the journey. They're hard to shake off because we tend to hold onto the negative longer than the positive. But if you can separate yourself from your "off" moments, they can be powerful learning experiences.

We often judge the quality of a decision based on the outcome, not taking into account the process behind the decision. When we make a bad decision, this outcome bias causes us to focus only on the negative outcome of going over budget, not being "smart enough," or any of the other lies we tell ourselves.

In those moments, if you can separate yourself from the outcome and trace the process back to why you made the decision, you can learn a lot about yourself, the situation, and how to avoid it in the future.

Were you stressed? In a time crunch? Bored? When you take a step back and evaluate your decision based on the process instead of the outcome, mistakes and setbacks stop being failures and become learning experiences. When you learn what makes you spend impulsively, veer away from your budget, or stay on the couch instead of doing the extra work, only then can you begin to gain control of your finances.

Today's Action Step:

- Write a plan for when life throws you a curveball or you mess up. You can do this on the Day 21 worksheet in the free workbook that accompanies this book. Find it at modernfrugality.com/debtfreeworkbook.

MOVING FORWARD

Now that you've finished these 21 days of tasks, you're perfectly poised to pay off your debt fast without any problems not covered in this book coming your way.

Just kidding. There are plenty of things I didn't cover that can pop up and derail you. But now, hopefully, you're equipped with the knowledge and skills to overcome them and succeed.

Your journey to pay off debt isn't done, and neither is your journey with this book. You can go back through it as many times as you need to, and you can revisit the workbook as you create new goals and learn more about yourself.

A story of someone paying off their debt in several months because of a windfall isn't nearly as captivating as a family of five that works for three years on a single income to become debt free. Yet, given the choice, we'd all take the windfall!

But I hope by now you've also come to realize, as I did, that the debt-free journey is just as important as the destination.

I don't regret going into debt for one second. The experience gave me everything I have today, and I know your experience will do similar things for you if you allow it to.

The most important thing you can do while paying off debt is to keep moving forward. A small step forward is still movement in the right direction. Small steps aren't sexy and it may look like you're going nowhere. But I guarantee every story you read or debt-free announcement you hear was preceded by a few big steps surrounded by a lot of small steps.

Once you understand that, there's no stopping you. You'll be able to fight through the setbacks, boredom, and difficulty that come with this journey, and you will pay off your debt for good.

The End

PAY OFF YOUR DEBT FOR GOOD

Want More?

Learn new and unique ways to save money and live simply at ModernFrugality.com and on every episode of the Frugal Friends Podcast. Available wherever you listen to podcasts.

And be sure to check out Jen's other books: The No-Spend Challenge Guide & Meal Planning on a Budget, available on Amazon Kindle and in paperback.

Made in the USA
Las Vegas, NV
30 January 2021

16819696R00111